PRAYER:
GOD AND YOU
ALONE

TRANSFORMING YOUR PRAYER LIFE
with Strategies, Action Tips, and Principles

Samuel O. Enyia

Dedication

I would like to dedicate this book to my children, Okechukwu, Chidirianyi, Ngozi, Onyinye, Amara, Chimaobi, and my mother-in-law, Catherine Nwagbara, who actively prays for us all daily.

Acknowledgements

I express my gratitude to Mr. Herbert Jackson for his invaluable insight, many probing questions, and suggestions he made on the content, structure, and focus of this book that contributed to make it better.

I thank you immensely, Mr. Samuel Umunna, for the enormous time you spent reading the manuscript and agreeing to write the foreword. I appreciate the suggestions you made on the content and particularly insightful comments you made in the foreword.

I am deeply grateful to my daughter, Amara,, for your very helpful editorial input. I thank my children Okechukwu, Chidirianyi, Ngozi, Onyinye, Amara, Chimaobi, and my grandson, Chukwuemeka, for their love and prayer support.

I am profoundly grateful to my wife, Irene, who is my partner in prayer and a prayer warrior, for her love, support, input and prayer covering as I wrote this book. Thank you, dear.

Finally, I thank God who, in spite of my weakness, encouraged, strengthened and guided me as I wrote this book.

Foreword

I have known Sam Enyia for over thirty years. We have been very close friends. Over that period, I was convinced that God has called him to the ministry of prayer and he has demonstrated his commitment to prayer very strongly and enthusiastically. When he asked me to write the foreword for this book, I was elated to do it.

Sam has masterfully crafted an excellent book that will change your prayer life. He has carefully articulated a comprehensive new perspective on prayer that will challenge, encourage, invigorate, and stimulate the interest of Christians who desire and seek to transform their prayer life.

This book is so engaging that I could not lay it down once I started reading the manuscript, and I have already applied the strategies and principles in it. Among other prayer books I have read, this one particularly has a unique perspective, insights, and action tips that will definitely transform your prayer life. I assure you that you will benefit tremendously from reading this book and your prayer life will definitely be transformed.

Samuel Umunna, President
Chicago South Chapter,
African Christian Fellowship, USA

Contents

Introduction

*P*rayer: God and You Alone, Transforming Your Prayer
Life with Strategies, Action Tips, and Principles, is
written to transform your prayer life dramatically, so you
can fully experience the power of God when you spend time
alone with Him. Above all, you will learn that the ultimate
outcome of prayer is to know that whatever the circumstances may be, God is still in control.

Sometimes, we hold too tight to the brakes in our lives.
We cling to our clenched fist. We cling to our past hurts and
fear. We cling to our comfort zone as if that is all there is.
We get entrenched in the status quo. We hold tight to what is
familiar even when we are not proud of it. We resist moving
forward. We blame everyone else for what has gone wrong,
but ourselves. When asked, we respond, "That's the way it
is for me. I would like it to be different, but it can't be now.
That's just the way it is and that's just the way I am. I'll have
to leave it that way. It is okay." No. It's not okay. You have
to let go and let God intervene in your life to make all the

necessary changes that will propel you to a level you have not been before in your prayer life.

When the Lord urged me to write this book, I was at the level in my prayer life when what mattered most was clinging to my hurts and fear, myself, my clenched fist, my comfort zone, and what was familiar, even with the things I was not proud of. I was afraid to open my hands, because I had experienced the agony of opening my hands and people would pound nails in them. But in spite of all this, the Lord challenged me to do it, because He said, "If you cling tightly to your own weaknesses, your faults, your shortcomings, and your past, to all the events, facts and situations which you would prefer to cut out of your own life, you're only hiding behind a hedge which everyone can see through."

Then the question emerged, how do I do this task? The answer was that I should go through the spectrum of learning the fundamental principles of prayer that I did not understand. What is prayer? Why should I spend time alone with God? How long should I pray? How long should I wait for God to answer? What if God answered, "Yes," "Delay," or "No," what should I do?

As I thought about these questions, more questions came up. What is the creative will of God? How does the will of God work in prayer? How will the Holy Spirit, and the Word of God, help me to release the prayer brakes in my life? Why should I study and pray the Word of God? What is my relationship and fellowship with God? How does it impact my prayer life?

While I searched for answers, other factors I did not know how to handle appeared. First is the fear factor. What is fear? How do I overcome negative fear? Second is the faith factor. What is faith? How do I activate and act on my faith? But wait a minute. I know that faith is important, however, how about obedience? How does it work?

While these questions kept me thinking, the most challenging question was how to pray to release the prayer brakes to transform our prayer lives. How do I forgive myself and others? How do I maintain consistent, effective, efficient, and disciplined prayer life with my daily busy work schedule, among other things I need to do at home and in the community?

I set up a prayer schedule and follow it for a while, and it's all in disarray, because of frequent unplanned changes. When this happens, I am afraid to make the necessary adjustments that will give me the most effective and satisfactory quality prayer life.

These perplexing concerns posed the greatest challenges to me. But I quickly realized that there are a few secrets about how to release the prayer brakes to transform your life. The first secret is not to be afraid about whether God is going to answer, "Yes," "Delay," or "No," but in being able to spend time alone with Him, listening to Him through the Word and being obedient to do what He has asked me to do.

Second is to learn to accept the changes God is about to introduce in my life.

Third, I learned that to accept God's challenges and changes in my life enables me to dissipate the fear of how God is going to answer. I also realized that the changes God makes in my life allow me to introduce variety and flexibility in my prayer life.

Fourth, I further realized that to release the prayer brakes required absolute surrender, trust, faith, dependence, and unwavering confidence in God, the Lord Jesus Christ, the Holy Spirit, and the authority of the Word.

Finally, I pray that as you read this book, the Lord will reveal to you something about Himself, His will, His Son, the Holy Spirit, the Word, and faith that will transform your life. I also pray that the Lord will enable you to learn what He intended for you to learn about yourself, your walk of faith, your relationship and fellowship with Him and others.

Even if what you read may not bring new knowledge to you, may He use it to clarify, reinforce, reenergize, and reengineer what you know already, May the Lord also strengthen your faith in Him and your prayer life. May you allow the Lord to help you make the most creative and meaningful use of your prayer time alone with Him. So let us together enter His presence in prayer.

Chapter One

What About Prayer?

**As the deer pants for streams of water, so my soul
pants for you, O God! My soul thirsts for God, for
the living God. When can I go and meet with God?
(Psalm 42:1-2)**

The most fascinating challenges about prayer are understanding what prayer is, the reasons we pray, how our
relationship and fellowship with God impact our prayer,
the will of God, the roles the Holy Spirit and the Word of
God play in our prayer, and the amazing expectations and
results we experience when we spend time alone with God.
A combination of these challenges and our determination to
diligently seek God's face constitute the fabric upon which
genuine prayer emerge.

As we approach God in that solitary moment, we ask
ourselves, what is this thing called prayer? What does it

mean? And why should we engage in it? The psalmist gives us a preview of what prayer is with a metaphor of a deer in the desert which is worn out and tired from chasing, running and roaming around, sometimes aimlessly, in a dry and arid desert land. The deer's tongue is dry. It is craving water and utterly desperate, and in search for a drink of water to quench a thirst, to refresh itself and regain its strength.

Like the deer metaphor, our souls must pant after God who is our stream of living water, from whom we can find a refreshing drink of water to satisfy our thirst. When we crave for God, when we desperately and diligently search for Him alone, then we will meet Him in prayer.

What is Prayer?

In search of what prayer is, some have defined it as speaking, communicating, questioning, listening, waiting, sharing and expressing our need to God. Prayer can be all of the above and much more. In short, prayer is the spoken or unspoken desire, the desperate longing, the hunger of our innermost search for God's attention, intervention, will and divine action to meet our needs. It is the hidden treasure of our innermost being. to meet with God. This definition leads us to answer the question: Why do we pray?

Reasons To Pray

There are several reasons why we need to pray. Some people have suggested that often dynamic prayer emerges as a result of desperate circumstances and conditions that challenge our life. Others suggest that prayer emerges from unresolved internal or external conflicts we may have with ourselves, with people, government, rules and legislations, health, family, those in authority, conflicts about our beliefs, values, customs, culture, our relationship with God and even sometimes, conflict with the unknown.

Often some of these conflicts drive us to God as our ultimate source of physical, emotional, psychological and spiritual deliverance. However, prayer should not only be the avenue for resolving our needs, but should also be a channel for seeking the will of God. Because we have a human nature that is frequently seeking for personal pleasure, gratification and in search of self-preservation, we gravitate toward God in search for closure. This matrix of human needs becomes the focus that urges us to pray. And as one need is satisfied, another need area emerges. The process becomes cyclical and more complex.

However, more specifically, these are other reasons we pray.

- Praying for protection from the devil and human desperation.

- Praying for forgiveness of our sins by God and by people
- Praying for God's wisdom, intellectual awareness and knowledge
- Praying for physical health, growth and strength
- Praying for personal comfort and courage
- Praying for physical, emotional and spiritual healing
- Praying for God's anointing
- Praying for safety and security
- Praying for God's guidance, instruction, and direction in decision making
- Praying for prosperity, abundance, wealth and riches
- Praying for justice from God
- Praying for physical, emotional, psychological, economic and spiritual well-being of others
- Praying for success, victory, and excellence in our life endeavors
- Praying for business, professional, and career success
- Praying to praise and glorify God
- Praying for patience and obedience

This list could go on and on, but our focus here is to ensure that in whatever combination the needs emerge, we understand that we can only take them to God when we pant and thirst after Him in that prayer time alone with expectations.

Our Prayer Expectations

But no matter how complex the matrix of our needs may be, God has given us the grace and fortitude to present our concerns to Him in prayer. And whether it is with a single prayer item or multiple items, our normal expectation is that God should alleviate or even eradicate our problem. However, we must understand that God's response to each circumstance is determined by Him alone. Sometimes God responds immediately to our needs and we are satisfied and pleased with Him. At other times, our prayer is not answered immediately, and we are discouraged and frustrated with God.

Consequently, we raise questions about God's power, authority, integrity, and credibility. We become very skeptical about the validity of God's Word. We are agitated and we wonder about what happens when God's answer is "Wait" or "No." We even become more cynical when our desires, interests and needs appear to be placed on hold. However, what we must understand is that God is still in control and His will and purpose for us must be accomplished by Him alone. Meanwhile, we must make sure that our personal relationship with God is intact. Let us find out how to do this.

Our Relationship With God

How God responds to our prayer and circumstances depends not only on Him alone, but also on our relationship with Him. Maintaining an intimate relationship with God is a necessary precondition for effective prayer life. Also God desires a relationship with us as His children. A relationship with Him enables us to interact and express our concerns and needs to Him. This relationship is made possible not by our own righteousness, but on our belief in what God did for us in Christ Jesus in His death and resurrection. As long as God maintains and sustains the relationship, we will always be His sons and daughters.

Our relationship with God is sealed in the redemptive sacrifice Jesus Christ made for us in His death. In this redemptive sacrifice, God reconciled us to Himself through Christ. This sacrifice that was done once and for all is not reversible and it cannot be revoked. In Romans 5:9-11, we read,

Since we have now been justified by his blood, how much more shall we be saved from God's wrath through him. For if when we were God's enemies, we were reconciled to him through the death of his son, how much more having been reconciled shall we be saved through his life. Not only is this so, but we also rejoice in God through our Lord Jesus Christ, through whom we have now received reconciliation.

In addition, our redemption in Christ brought the forgiveness of our sins and set us free from the guilt of sin and opened the door for us to have access to God in prayer. Colossians 1:14, reads, "...In whom we have redemption and the forgiveness of sins."

The same promise is reinforced in Ephesians 1:17, "In whom we have redemption through his blood, the forgiveness of sins, in accordance with the riches of God's grace that he lavished on us with all wisdom, and understanding."

Our Fellowship With God

While our relationship with God is a precondition for effective prayer life, our fellowship with Him is also important. To have fellowship with God requires us to have an understanding of the rules of engagement during our fellowship times. We can have fellowship with God by studying His Word, worshiping in praise, laying down our burdens, confessing our sins and agreeing that He is all powerful and in control of everything about us.

To have fellowship with God also means we have to act in humility, faith, trust, obedience and confidence and in submission to His authority. In return, we receive all the blessings and benefits that come with our fellowship. And whereas our relationship with God is irrevocable, when we break the rules of fellowship engagement due to sin or disobedience, God will always restore our fellowship with

Him the moment we confess our sins. 1 John 1:8-9, "If we claim that we are without sin, we deceive ourselves and the truth is not in us. If we confess our sins, he is faithful and just and will forgive us our sins and purify us from all unrighteousness." Once our fellowship is restored we are ready to engage in prayer conversation, listening and sharing those innermost desires of our lives.

Why Tell God What He Already Knows?

We now know the importance of relationship and fellowship with God in our prayer life. We also know that God is Almighty, all-knowing, and all-powerful. He knows all about us and all our needs. Why do we have to tell Him what He already knows? Why doesn't He give us what we need without our asking, seeking and knocking? These are the questions about God and prayer that are so mysterious, but the answer lies in our understanding of the creative will of God. How this works is next.

Questions for Reflection

Instruction: After you have read this chapter, take a moment to reflect on the following questions and comment on them to assess your understanding of it.

1. What is prayer?

_____

_____

_____

2. What are your most compelling reasons for praying?

_____

_____

_____

3. Describe your expectations from God when you pray.

_____

_____

_____

4. How valuable to you is maintaining a relationship and fellowship with God?

_____

_____

_____

5. Explain why prayer should play a very important role in your life.

_____

_____

_____

6. Are you satisfied with your answers?

_____

_____

_____

7. Would you feel comfortable sharing your answers with a friend or in a group?

_____

_____

_____

Chapter Two

Knowing God's Creative Will

This is what the Lord says - your Redeemer, who formed you in the womb, I am the Lord, who alone stretched out the heavens, who spread out the earth by myself.
(Isaiah 44:24)

Yes, and from the ancient days, I am he. No one can deliver out of my hand. When I act, who can reverse it?
(Isaiah 43:13)

Knowing the creative will of God will help you understand its impact on your prayer life. Nothing about you will be possible if you have no knowledge of who designed and executed a plan for your life. And the entire process began in Genesis 1 & 2. The creative act could not be possible without a design, a plan and a will. It was God's will to create the universe. It was His will to create man and redeem him from sin. If God has not willed it, it will not be. God's will means "to be," "to be effective," and "to come to be." And that is how you came to be. It is important for you to know that God acted alone in this creative process.

Another aspect of God's will is immutable. God's will does not change, because God does not change. He remains the same through eternity. But frequently, changes in your own circumstances and experiences occur. Although God is capable of acting alone without human assistance, He chooses to act through your circumstances, and through these reveal His will. So our prayer should not only be to ask God to provide our needs, but ask Him to fulfill His will by meeting those needs.

Knowing God's Creative Act

How God's independent creative act affect you is accounted for in Genesis 1:26,

> Then God said, "Let us make man in our image, in our likeness, and let them rule over the fish of the sea, and the birds of the air, over the livestock, over all the earth, and over all the creatures that move along the ground."

In the passage, God determined that man must be created in His image and likeness. He also gave man the authority over all creatures in the sea, air and land. But God's decision to create man was manifested in Genesis 1:27, "So God created man in His own image, in the image of God he created him, male and female he created them." However, the actual execution of the creation of man was completed in Genesis 2:7,

> The Lord God formed the man from the dust of the ground and breathed into his nostrils the breath of life, and the man became a living being.

God's Provision for Quality Life

In this creative process, God acted alone. He also acted alone in providing all the necessary ingredients for man to experience maximum, comfortable, and quality living.

God also provided the man with a living environment that was ideal for fulfilling his physical, psychological, social, economic, intellectual and spiritual needs.

In Genesis 2:8-25, all these special provisions were complete. For the man's personal pleasure in the environment, God took the following action.

1. Now, the Lord God planted a garden in the east of Eden, and there he put the man he had formed.

2. God provided the man with all species of trees that were attractive and pleasing to the eyes, and also good for food.
3. God provided the man with water from the river that flowed out of Eden to water the garden. The water was divided into four rivers, Pishon, Gihon, Tigris, and Euphrates. These rivers provided abundant water for both irrigating the vegetation, and for drinking.
4. God provided the man with a source of financial stability and wealth.

Genesis 2:11, reads,

The name of the first river is Pishon, it winds through the entire land of Havilah, where there is gold (the gold of the land is good, aromatic,resin and onyx are also there). The name of the second river is Gihon, it winds through the entire land of Cush. The name of the third river is Tigris, it runs around the east side of Asshur. And the fourth river is Euphrates.

5. God provided man with the tree of life in the middle of the garden and the tree of the knowledge of good and evil
6. God put the man in control (man was in charge) and authorized him to cultivate and keep this beautiful, quality life and world he created for the man

The climax of the level of comfortable living God had planned for the man was to give him a woman companion and helper as his wife. God also granted him the freedom to eat from all the trees in the garden except the tree of the knowledge of good and evil. In Genesis 2:16-17, God issued His command:

And the Lord God commanded the man, "You are free to eat from the garden, but you must not eat from the tree of the knowledge of good and evil, for when you eat of it, you will surely die."

God's Specific Instructions to The Man

With the command, God specified clearly His instructions about what to eat and what not to eat. He also was assertive in clearly prescribing consequences of disobedience. God had completed His creative act and it is left to the man to respond to God's expression of love to him. Unfortunately, man failed woefully at his first opportunity to exercise his freedom. He made the wrong choice by disobeying God's command. Consequently, his disobedience resulted in man's fall, separation, excommunication, and a ban from the presence of God. What happened?

The Serpent's Visit With The Woman

Man's act of disobedience began with the woman God had given to him as a companion and wife. The woman had engaged in conversation with a crafty serpent. The serpent has been referred to in different parts of the Bible as Satan, the devil, the wicked one, the tempter, the dragon, the evil one, Belial, Beelzebub, etc. This is the one that deceived the woman.

The Serpent: The First Journalist

During the conversation between the woman and the serpent in Genesis 3:1-2, the serpent introduced the topic of conversation in a subtle, appealing process, like a stalagmite that drips a little drop at a time until it is fully formed and engulfs its subject. Consequently, the cumulative effect of the serpent's conversation ate gradually into the woman's mind until she was worn out and defeated.

The serpent's visit and strategy had a profound impact on the woman, in the same way a journalist in pursuit of news influences the newsmaker. He knew that the woman was a potential newsmaker. He used the power of suggestion effectively on her. He used his professional strategy of a leading question to suggest a preferred response to the woman. The woman responded according to the serpent's leading question. The suggestion cast doubt on the credibility and authority of God's Word.

Here is the progression of their conversation in Genesis 3:1-5,

The serpent:

Question: "Did God really say, "You must not eat from any tree in the garden?"

The woman:

Answer: "The woman said to the serpent, "We may eat fruit from trees in the garden, but God did say, you must not eat fruit from the tree that is in the middle of the garden, and you must not touch it, or you will die. (a long answer)

The serpent:

Comment "You will not surely die," the serpent said to the woman. For God knows that when you eat of it, your eyes will be opened, and you will be like God, knowing good and evil."

The woman:

Answer: (surprised) Oh really!

With this conversation, the serpent cast doubt in the woman's mind about the authority and authenticity of God's Word. The tragedy is that what the woman knew about God's command was sufficient for her to reject the serpent's lies. She had an accurate knowledge of God's instructions. She understood the specific instructions. She knew all the facts. She memorized the instructions and recalled them. In spite of all these, the woman made a conscious choice to disobey God's first command, and instead obeyed the serpent's first deceit. She chose the serpent's opinion over God's facts and truth. The serpent's alternative was more attractive to the woman.

> "When the woman saw that the fruit of the tree was good for food, and pleasing to the eye, and also desirable for gaining wisdom, she took some and ate it. She also gave some to her husband who was with her, and he ate it."

Man, Participant in Disobedience

Although the woman was the serpent's target, the man also was a conscious participant in the act of disobedience. Apparently, the woman persuaded the man to eat the forbidden fruit. In other words, man's first attempt to exercise his freedom and will was an act of disobedience. He made a selfish choice by ignoring the relationship and fellowship he originally had with God. This act destroyed the original peaceful and harmonious relationship. And the consequence was devastating. He acquired for himself, physical, social, psychological and spiritual separation from God. He lost everything and brought himself shame and fear. Read this in Genesis 3:8-10,

Then the man and his wife heard the sound of the Lord God as he was walking in the garden in the cool of the day, and they hid from the Lord God among the trees of the garden. But the Lord God called to the man. Where are you? ...He answered, I heard you in the garden and I was afraid because I was naked, so I hid.

Consequence for Disobedience

Because God does not tolerate disobedience, man had to bear the full responsibility for his act of disobedience, and he paid dearly for it with the following restrictions. He lost Eden in Genesis 3:22-24,

And the Lord God said, the man has become like one of us, knowing good and evil. He must not be allowed to reach out his hand and take also from the tree of life and eat, and live forever. So the Lord God banished him from the Garden of Eden to work the ground from which he had been taken. After he drove the man out, he placed on the east side of the Garden of Eden, cherubim and a flaming sword flashing back and forth to guard the way to the tree of life.

By this action, God drove man away to protect His holiness. And this was the beginning of a broken, damaged, and ruined relationship between God and man. This ruined relationship made it impossible for man to pray. The implication for us is that in our damaged relationship with God, the door was slammed shut. This one act of disobedience shut us all out of God's presence. Something different had to happen for us to return to God, and therefore be able to pray to Him.

We have to acknowledge and agree with God that our disobedience works contrary to God's will for us, because all our ways and behavior have become completely sinful and anti God. Genesis 6:5 reads,

The Lord saw how great man's wickedness on the earth had become, and that every inclination of the thoughts of his heart was only evil all the time.

Also in Isaiah 53:6, we read, "We all like sheep have gone astray, each of us have turned to his own way." Under this condition, we could not redeem ourselves unless God intervened for us. So God designed a plan and a process for us to return to Him. Here is how.

God Restores Man to Himself

Although man's first act of disobedience separated him from God, God acted alone to reach out to man to restore the damaged relationship. But God's final act of restoration was demonstrated through the death and resurrection of our Lord Jesus Christ, His son. In other words, God reconciled man to Himself. Romans 5:9-11,

Since we have now been justified by his blood, how much more shall we be saved from God's wrath, through him, For if when we were God's enemies, we were reconciled to him through the death of his son, how much more having been reconciled, shall we be saved through his life. Not only is this so, but we also rejoice in God through our Lord Jesus Christ, through whom we have now received reconciliation.

This act of reconciliation began when God invited man to Himself in John 3:16, which reads,

For God so loved the world that he gave his one and only Son, that whoever believes in him shall not perish but have eternal life.

God's Invitation to Restoration

Here God acted alone by reaching out to us with an invitation to restoration and new life when we accept Jesus, His Son, as our Lord and Savior. It is up to us to accept or reject God's gift of salvation. If we accept, we are saved from the wrath of sin, but if we reject, we subject ourselves to eternal judgment. Read this in John 3:17-18,

For God did not send his Son into the world to condemn the world, but to save the world through him. Whoever believes in him is not condemned, but whoever does not believe in him stands condemned already because he has not believed in the name of God's one and only son.

This is the test. Finally, if you believe in Christ Jesus, you make your will compatible to the will of God. Then your relationship and fellowship is restored and you are ready to spend that time alone with God in prayer. Next, to spend that time alone with God, we need to know how to pray according to God's will.

Questions for Reflection

Instruction: Respond to these questions about the will of God and the fall.

1. What is your understanding about God's creative will?

_____

_____

_____

_____

2. How did God manifest His creative act?

_____

_____

_____

_____

3. What caused the fall of man?

_____

_____

_____

_____

4. What was the outcome of Satan's visit with the woman?

— — — — — — — — — — — — — — — — — — —

— — — — — — — — — — — — — — — — — — —

— — — — — — — — — — — — — — — — — — —

— — — — — — — — — — — — — — — — — — —

5. Explain the consequence of disobedience to God?

— — — — — — — — — — — — — — — — — — —

— — — — — — — — — — — — — — — — — — —

— — — — — — — — — — — — — — — — — — —

— — — — — — — — — — — — — — — — — — —

6. How did the act of restoration take place?

— — — — — — — — — — — — — — — — — — —

— — — — — — — — — — — — — — — — — — —

— — — — — — — — — — — — — — — — — — —

— — — — — — — — — — — — — — — — — — —

7. Would you feel free sharing your answer with others?
   Why?

_____

_____

_____

_____

Chapter Three

Pray: God's Will

In the same way, the Spirit helps us in our weakness. We do not know what we ought to pray for, but the Spirit himself intercedes for us with groans that words cannot express. And he who searches our hearts, knows the mind of the Spirit, because the Spirit intercedes for the saints in accordance with God's will.
(Romans 8:26-27)

Get Help from The Holy Spirit

The challenge of praying according to God's will is a task we must submit to the leading of the Holy Spirit. God made clear the enabling function of the Holy Spirit in our prayer. And we need to understand the reasons the Holy Spirit must be involved in our prayer life.

1. We must acknowledge our weakness
2. We do not know what to pray for
3. We do not know what to say or how to say it
4. The Holy Spirit intercedes for us
5. We must surrender ourselves to the control of the Holy Spirit
6. We must relinquish all personal power and humble ourselves before God
7. We must allow the Holy Spirit to take control of our needs, desires, and thoughts so He can act on them as He intercedes for us
8. The Holy Spirit prays for us according to God's will

When you understand these reasons and submit yourself to the control of the Holy Spirit, you acknowledge the fact that praying according to the will of God is indeed not what you do by yourself, instead it is God acting on your behalf through the Holy Spirit. In other words, if you do not yield to the Holy Spirit, you may be making a fruitless effort trying to pray.

How refreshing it is to know that the Holy Spirit is interceding for you. He searches your heart, knows what is in it. The Holy Spirit knows the mind of God and what pleases Him. He takes all your weaknesses and submits them to God's will and speaks to God on your behalf. What an awesome responsibility the Holy Spirit has taken for you.

And remember, the Lord Jesus Christ had promised that the Holy Spirit will take what is His and make it known to you. John 16:13-14 reads,

But when he, the Spirit of truth comes, he will guide you into all truth. He will not speak on his own, he will speak only what he hears and he will tell you what is yet to come. He will bring glory to me by taking from what is mine and making it known to you.

When you allow the Holy Spirit to intercede in your prayer, He will bring to your mind all the truth from the Word of God and guide you to understand the truth. As you begin to pray, allow the Holy Spirit to reveal to you what He hears from the Lord, and this He will reveal to you through His Word. Also understand that the Holy Spirit has a prophetic authority to tell you what is yet to happen in your life. As you pray, be prepared to accept the counsel of the Holy Spirit, who prays for you according to God's will.

We will learn more about praying according to God's will with two very powerful examples. The first is Jesus' prayer at Gethsemane, and the second is Hannah's prayer for a son.

Jesus' Prayer at Gethsemane

The ultimate example of praying according to God's will is the prayer of our Lord Jesus Christ at Gethsemane, recorded in Matthew 26:36-42; Mark 14:32-36; Luke 22:40-42: Jesus went with His disciples to Gethsemane in preparation for His death on the cross. When they arrived at Gethsemane, Jesus began to experience a compelling urge to pray. This urge emerged out of desperation, grief, agony, distress and a deep sense of what appeared to be an impending predicament. Matthew 26:36:

> Then Jesus went with his disciples to a place called Gethsemane, and he said to them, "Sit here while I go over there and pray. He took Peter and the sons of Zebedee along with him and he began to be sorrowful and troubled. Then he said to them, "My soul is overwhelmed with sorrow to the point of death. Stay here and keep watch with me. Going a little farther, he fell with his face to the ground and prayed, "My Father, if it is possible, may this cup be taken from me. Yet not as I will but as you will."....He went away a second time and prayed, "My Father, if it is not possible for this cup to be taken away, unless I drink it, may your will be done." (Jesus prayed the same thing for a third time.)

Jesus Surrenders Power

The most fascinating aspect of Jesus' Gethsemane experience was that it was an embodiment of ultimate human predicament. It was the only one of its kind in the history of humanity and it could never be repeated. No one else has suffered such humiliation. None before Him and none after. In His prayer, Jesus demonstrated ultimate dependence on the will of God. He relinquished all power, authority, and divine attributes, and took up all human qualities, assuming a condition of weakness. He experienced grief, pain, distress, humiliation, ridicule, rejection, frustration, depression, abandonment, and shame. But His weakness on the cross was transformed into power at His resurrection, by which humanity was reconciled to God through Him.

God Had an Eternal Plan

At Gethsemane, Jesus, in expressing His human qualities, was looking at a present despicable condition. He would prefer not to drink the cup of agony and He was not afraid to express His opinion and desire, but God had an eternal redemptive plan. While Jesus' prayer did not change God's plan, it prepared Him to absolutely depend on His Father's will.

As you learn about praying according to God's will, you must understand that God will answer according to His will.

And that your prayer will not alter God's plan. Jesus set this prime example for us to follow in His steps and join Him in praying, "Father, if it is not possible for this cup to be taken away, unless I drink it, may your will be done"

Questions for Reflection

Instruction: React to the questions about the Holy Spirit's role in relation to praying according to God's will.

1. How does the Holy Spirit function in us when we pray?

_____

_____

_____

2. Why does the Holy Spirit pray according to God's will?

_____

_____

_____

3. How did Jesus' experience at Gethsemane involve praying according to God's will?

_____

_____

_____

4. How would praying according to God's will impact your prayer?

_____

_____

_____

5. Will you recommend praying according to God's will? Why?

_____

_____

_____

6. Would you feel free sharing how the Holy Spirit worked in your prayer life?

_____

_____

_____

Chapter Four

Pray and Wait Factor

Wait for the Lord, be strong and take heart and wait for the Lord.
(Psalm 27:14)

One of the most frustrating aspects of prayer is the waiting factor. We pray expecting the answer now. We are in a hurry. We don't like to wait for anything. We want instant everything, but God says wait. You can hurry as much as you want, but you can hurry and wait. When we don't get our preferred instant answer, we are frustrated and sometimes angry. But when we finally give in the negative attitude kicks in. And we ask, "God, now you said wait, but how long?" and God says again, "You can wait until I act." Wow! Our test case for the pray and wait factor is Hannah's encounter with God in I Samuel.

Hannah and Her Family

The story about Hannah's encounter with God is told in 1 Samuel 1. Hannah had a husband, Elkanah, who had a second wife, Peninnah. Peninnah had children, but Hannah had no children. Elkanah and his wives lived in Ramathaim-Zophim.

Every year, Elkanah went with his family to Shiloh to worship and make sacrifices to the Lord Almighty before Eli the priest and his sons, Hophni and Phenihas. At the place of sacrifice, Elkanah gave Peninnah and her children portions of the sacrifice, enough for all of them, but he gave a double portion to Hannah because he loved her. But the Lord had closed Hannah's womb. (1 Samuel 1:4-6). Who was Hannah and what happened to her?

Hannah Prays, God Says Wait

The conditions under which Hannah's prayer emerged give us insight into what kind of a woman she was. The Bible described Hannah as a deeply troubled woman. Her life was devastated socially, culturally, and emotionally. She was depressed and distressed. The Lord closed her womb. She had a rival woman in her family. She was continually provoked by Peninnah for many years. She was vulnerable and wept bitterly, but she was a praying woman. The only thing she had left was her spiritual strength and dependence on the Lord.

In spite of all this, Hannah summoned up courage to go to the Lord who closed her womb, to pray. All human intervention was inadequate, even the comfort from her husband was inadequate. Her feelings of hurt, rejection, ridicule, and distress were the matrix that propelled her to seek help from the Lord. Listen to her husband,

And because the Lord had closed her womb, her rival kept provoking her in order to irritate her. This went on year after year; Whenever Hannah went up to the house of the Lord, her rival provoked her till she wept and would not eat. Elkanah her husband will say to her, Hannah why are you weeping? Why don't you eat? Why are you downhearted? Don't I mean more to you than ten sons?
(1 Samuel 1:6-8).

Elkanah's Inadequate Help

Although Elkanah tried to comfort Hannah, he misunderstood Hannah's real condition. He analyzed the problem in human terms. For Elkanah, the quality of their relationship was more important than having many children, but he was also naïve because he neglected the cultural implications of not having a son. His statement suggested a break in social and cultural norms. Indeed, in the culture of the Hebrews, not having a son was an abomination, looked unto as a curse. And for Hannah, the thought of not having a son placed her in the class of social and cultural outcast. But the expression of love and comfort from Elkanah was undermined by Peninnah's unrelenting provocation and ridicule.

When God created man and woman, He placed the woman in a special position of honor to be the one who bears a child in her womb. For women, it is a thing of joy. This special status gave a woman a sense of fulfillment, social, cultural and emotional satisfaction. For God to close Hannah's womb must have been devastatingly disappointing. And Hannah's search for help from God was uncertain. But she had an unwavering faith in God, who had the power to call things that are not as though they were.

God Will Not Act Before His Time

But God was not unaware of Hannah's misery. However, Hannah's misery and predicament will not rush God into action. God will wait until His time to act on Hannah's condition. God saw the big picture about Hannah and her family. While God was looking to raise a leader for Israel, Hannah was preoccupied with her own immediate need to have a son. Did God know about Hannah's affliction, provocation and broken-heartedness? Yes, He knew all that. How true the scripture is in Isaiah 55:8-9,

For my thoughts are not your thoughts, neither are your ways my ways, declares the Lord. As the heavens are higher than the earth, so are my ways higher than your ways and my thoughts than your thoughts.

Although Hannah was preoccupied with her misery, she understood that she must depend only on the Lord to come to her rescue. She understood that her thoughts were not enough in themselves to change anything. She also understood that her ways were different from God's ways, and so she must depend on God alone. Yes, her condition was depressing, but she was determined to seek answers from the Lord. She knew that only the all-powerful God who closed her womb was the one to open it. And she had to wait, but how long?

Eli The Priest Misunderstands Hannah

Often we misunderstand someone else's condition. Sometimes we misunderstand other people's predicaments, because we do not care or because of ignorance, our ego, selfishness, pride, jealousy, envy, or whatever the reason, we are not alone, but this also cannot be a justification. Even Eli the priest in Shiloh, where Hannah was praying, misunderstood Hannah's prayer and alluded that she must have been drinking alcohol and therefore was drunk. Read this,

In bitterness of soul Hannah wept much and prayed to the Lord.. And as she kept on praying to the Lord, Eli observed her mouth, Hannah was praying in her heart and her lips were moving but her voice was not heard. Eli thought she was drunk, and said to her, how long will you keep on getting drunk? Get rid of your wine.
(1 Samuel 1:10, 12, &13)

Despite the fact that Eli misunderstood Hannah's prayer, she was convinced that the priest's interpretation would not deter her from her focus on God, even though she did not know how long it was going to take God to answer. She had been going with her family year after year to worship and make sacrifices. And God was waiting for all those years for Hannah to pray repeatedly before He acted. God will wait for His time, even though He had predetermined to do His will for her. Read this,

But do not forget this one thing, dear friends. With the Lord, a day is like a thousand years and a thousand years are like a day (II Peter 3:8)

Also read Galatians 4:4,

But when the time had fully come, God sent His Son, born of a woman, born under law to redeem

those under the law that we might receive the full rights of sons.

God chooses to do His will according to His own time. He does not depend on our time. Our time is chronological and linear but God's time is timeless. He will act at the fullness of His time. Our prayer and urging may not necessarily rush God into action, but our prayer places us before Him in fellowship.

In Hannah's case, God waited until she expressed agreement with Him in prayer. God initiated something in her and He waited for her to respond in prolonged prayer encounters that lasted for years. Even though the will of God governed Hannah's prayer, her prayer did not change His will. And that is the reason for us to pray, "Your will be done, O God."

It's Been So Long

Although Hannah was ready to wait for God to act, she was not sure how long it would take. But she was determined to wait. She would not leave any stone unturned. She did not want to take chances. The possibility that God would forget her was ruled out, even though the prolonged time of uncertainty was a legitimate concern. She did not hesitate to call God's attention to her condition; she prayed, "Lord, it's been so long." The length of time must have been the reason it seemed that God had forgotten her, but for God, length of time made no difference.

That God will wait until the fullness of His time does not mean that God has forgotten, even if many years have elapsed. In many ways, we are like Hannah. We pray and expect immediate answers, and when we don't get instant answers, we ask why it has taken so long. But we learn from Hannah that we cannot rush God into action. Instead, we must keep praying and waiting until it is the fullness of God's time. When that time comes, God will act and He will act decisively.

Hannah Prays for God's Will

Prayer that seeks God's will must submit to God's requirement that we ask according to God's will. This is precisely what Hannah did. Hannah presented a selfless request to the Lord. She took her self out as the center of interest and placed all focus on how to serve, honor and praise God. Hannah's request contained a vow in which she invoked the will of God. The vow was entered into in 1 Samuel 1:11, which reads,

And she made a vow saying, O Lord Almighty, if you will only look upon your servant's misery and remember me and not forget your servant, but give her a son, then I will give him to the Lord for all the days of his life, and no razor will ever be used on his head.

Hannah's Two-Part Petition

Hannah's prayer began with a two-fold contract. The first part invoked the will of God, and the second part specified Hannah's responsibility. For Hannah, God's will superseded her asking. Her prayer allowed her to surrender and submit to the will of God.

A Selfless Prayer

The second part of Hannah's prayer is one of the greatest examples of selfless prayer. She was not thinking about herself. She was more concerned about how to serve and praise God than personal need. Her prayer for a son who would serve God all the days of his life was paramount. She recognized that she did not possess the power to change anything by herself. She was committed to challenge God to act on her petition. With the vow, Hannah bound herself to a commitment and a responsibility to keep her vow. She was accountable to herself and to God to comply with her vow. What she said in effect was, "Lord, if it is your will to give me a son, it is my will to give him back to you, to serve you all the days of his life." What a prayer!

God To Remember Hannah

Elkanah lay with his wife, and the Lord remembered her. So in the course of time, Hannah conceived and gave birth to a son. She named him Samuel, saying, Because I asked the Lord for Him (I Samuel 1:19-20)

A unique phenomenon about Hannah's prayer was her appeal to God to remember her. "If you will only look upon your servant and remember me and not forget your servant." Hannah's prayer zeroed in on God's ability to look and remember her. Hannah's prayer reminded her that God is not capable of forgetting the very things He created, because He is all-knowing. However, God has no need to remember anything, because for Him there is no difference between the past, present, and future.

The outcome of Hannah's prayer was that after many years of misery, provocation, ridicule, humiliation, and childlessness, God gave her a son. She named him Samuel, which means, "a child of asking." This name was to remind Hannah about her encounter with the God who closed her womb and the God who acted in His time and the God who says, "Hush!" when we are in a hurry.

Hannah Lets Go and Lets God

You may be familiar with the persisting attitude common among us. We bring a request or a problem to God. We prescribe how we want God to answer. Then we get up and pack the whole bag of problems we just prayed about and move right away, worrying and trying to solve the problems by ourselves. We don't let go and we don't let God act. But Hannah let go and let God act, and God acted in His time.

We cannot pray and worry, because praying and worrying will not really change anything. After Hannah prayed thoroughly, she went her way and ate and her face was no longer sad. She laid her burdens at the feet of the Lord, and left them there. And she worshipped the Lord there. Hannah prayed and worshipped. So we also must pray and worship, not pray and worry. Remember praying and worrying are mutually exclusive.

Hannah made a lifelong, selfless commitment to the Lord. She did not say, if God gave her a son, she would take good care of him and praise God for him. No, Hannah was willing and precise in her vow, to give him back to God to serve Him all his entire life.

Hannah Keeps Her Vow

After Samuel was born, Hannah did not go to the temple with her husband and family to worship and make sacrifices, until Samuel was weaned. She said to her husband, "After the boy is weaned, I will take him and present him before the Lord and he will live there always." (I Samuel 1:22)

Hannah remembered her vow and acted on it. She brought Samuel to Eli, the priest in Shiloh, and sacrificed to the Lord, and she said to him, "As surely as you live, my lord, I am the woman who stood here beside you, praying to the Lord. I prayed for this child, and the Lord has granted me what I asked of Him. So now, I give him to the Lord. For his whole life he will be given over to the Lord." And she worshipped the Lord there." (I Samuel 1:26-29)

God had done His part. He fulfilled His promise and Hannah kept her word. She kept her vow. Hannah prayed to God in anguish. She waited for years before God answered. God acted in His time. What an amazing relationship and fellowship with God. Can you pray and wait for the Lord to act in His time? This is your challenge.

You'll Have To Wait

Well, there is another dimension to pray and wait. Hannah prayed for many years for a son before the Lord answered her prayer. You might say, yes that was Hannah, but what about you? What if you asked God for something you desperately need now, as Hannah did, and God said, "You'll Have to Wait"? What do you do? Let us read Psalm 130:5-6,

I wait for the Lord, my soul waits, and in his word, I put my hope. My soul waits for the Lord, more than watchmen wait for the morning, more than watchmen wait for the morning.

Principle Of Divine Delay

This scripture is teaching us about indefinite waiting time. You have to wait as long as God has determined, as expressed in His principle of divine delay. This principle is encapsulated in the idea that you ought to be prepared to wait as long as necessary. But we can benefit from this principle. How?

What The Principle Of Divine Delay Teaches

- Prayer is about waiting
- Prayer is like fishing. You throw your bait and wait
- Prayer is the poetry of waiting. You repeat the rhyme and rhythm and wait
- Prayer is not about bartering. Not bargaining or deal making
- Prayer is not about comparative or competitive advantage. You trade your commodity and exchange what you have an advantage over another's goods

Who Are You Waiting For?

- Waiting for people (lazy people, type A, B, C, and all other types, the good, bad, gossipers, cowards, hateful, friendly, unfriendly, proud, arrogant, uncaring, greedy, jealous, unloving, unfaithful, ugly, pretty, handsome, beautiful, hot tempered, cool tempered, etc.)
- Ultimate waiting is on God, who is in control of all things.

How Long Is The Waiting?

- Until the fullness of time (Galatians 4:4)
- In due time (I Timothy 2:6)
- In God's time economy (I Peter 3:8-9, a day = a thousand years
- Until God's will, purpose, and promise is complete. Such a time can be real long, trying, testing, painful, challenging, frustrating, and depressing. But you are waiting for God by faith, until He acts on behalf of those who wait for Him (Isaiah 64:6)

What Are The Benefits of Waiting?

- It invigorates, renews, replenishes, and revives our strength in the Lord. It enables us to walk and not faint

- Enables us to run and not get weary
- Enables us to rise up on wings as eagles
- God's purpose is fulfilled in our life during our waiting period

The Meaning of Prayer and Waiting

- We must allow God to teach us His Divine Principle of Delay
- We must allow Him to teach us His Decree Principle of saying No, as was the case with the Apostle Paul in II Corinthians 12:9, "My grace is sufficient for you, for my power is made perfect in weakness. Therefore, I will boast all the more gladly about my weaknesses, so that Christ's power may rest on me."
- Even though Jesus' disciples, Mary, and Martha thought that Jesus' coming to Lazarus was too late, they did not recognize that Jesus had the authority and power to resurrect that which was dead. In other words, Jesus was not in a hurry. He took His time to fulfill God's purpose
- Praying and waiting are about being made in the likeness of Christ and being transformed and complete in Him.

So, do not get weary in waiting, because in due time you will receive your benefits.

Wait Wait Wait for God

Questions for Reflection

Instruction: Provide your insight on praying and waiting.

1. What does praying and waiting mean to you?

_____

_____

_____

2. Why do we have a hard time waiting after we have prayed?

_____

_____

_____

3. What are the benefits of waiting?

_____

_____

_____

4. How does the principle of Divine Delay work?

_____

_____

_____

5. How would the way Hannah handled waiting on God apply to you?

_____

_____

_____

6. Will you feel free to share your experience with waiting on God with others? Why?

_____

_____

_____

Chapter Five

ASK, ASK, ASK

Ask and it will be given to you; seek and you will find; knock and the door will be opened to you. For everyone who asks receives, he who seeks finds; and to him who knocks, the door will be opened. (Matthew 7:7-8)

L earning how to ask and receive from God is so pivotal for you to understand its dynamics. After you have read this very important chapter, you will begin to apply these principles of asking and receiving that will help you transform your prayer.

These principles include,

1. Reasons for asking
2. How to ask and receive
3. Ask, Ask, Ask

4. Ask for what is good
5. Ask in relationship and fellowship
6. Don't ask with wrong motives
7. Don't ask with a stubborn attitude
8. Ask while you remain in Him
9. Ask with confidence
10. Ask through the Holy Spirit
11. Ask in the name of Jesus

Reasons for Asking

The principle of asking for anything and everything from God is a lifelong activity that will not change any time soon. Even when we decide not to ask, or ask and don't receive now, must not stop us from asking again and again. Whatever the outcome, the principle remains unchanged. And as long as we live, this phenomenon will continue to operate in our daily lives. But the unique thing about it is that asking opens a communication opportunity for us to interact among ourselves and with God.

Some of the reasons for asking from God are for our own benefits to,

1. strengthen our relationship and fellowship with God through prayer
2. teach us not to give up, even if we do not receive what we have asked for now

3. demonstrate our dependence on God as the ultimate provider of our needs
4. demonstrate our confidence in Him as the only one we must trust
5. teach us how to persevere even when we have to wait for a long time
6. train and discipline us to anchor our faith in Him
7. enable us to believe His Word and pray His Word.
8. worship and praise Him through our asking
9. convince us that His will is for our best interest.

Once we have resolved in our minds that these reasons operate to benefit us, we are assured that we have nothing to lose by asking God, but we have everything to gain. We gain His love, kindness, joy, peace, riches, wealth, victory, compassion, mercy, health, healing, security, protection, wisdom, power, understanding grace, and above all, eternal life. These reasons lead us to the path of learning how to ask and receive.

Principle # 1: Ask, Ask, Ask

The principle to ask, ask, ask, is based on the premise that if you ask, and do not receive now, ask again and again, because you have nothing to lose by asking. Our Lord Jesus drove this principle home by saying that it is better to ask repeatedly until you receive. You should not be ashamed, even when the answer now is no. In other words, do not give up. He made it clear that the precondition for asking and receiving anything from God depends on our persistence. We are not to ask only once, twice, three times, but ask until we have asked thoroughly.

Principle # 2: Ask For What Is Good

Although the Lord commanded us to ask repeatedly until we receive, He also mandated us to ask for what is good. He illustrated this principle of asking for what is good with a natural father-son relationship. Matthew 7:9 reads,

Which of you, if his son asks for bread, will give him a stone? Or if he asks for a fish, will give him a snake? If you, then, though you are evil, know how to give good gifts to your children, how much more will your Father in heaven give good gifts to those who ask him!

The mandate of this principle requires a son to ask for what will have good benefit to him. In this case, he asks for bread. He knows that bread is good for food and will strengthen his physical body. Sarcastically, the Lord asks how can a father whose son asked for bread give him a stone, or if he asks for fish give him a snake? It does not make sense. It is cruel and unnatural. Bread and fish are good for food. In contrast, stone and snake will hurt the son. If the son swallowed a stone or ate a poisonous snake, he could die. The only option his father has is to respond by giving his son what is good.

In other words, if an evil natural father could have the judgment to give his son a good thing, then there is no doubt that our Father in heaven will give us every good thing when we ask Him. Consequently, the asking, giving, and receiving are done both for our benefit and to the glory of God. So, when you ask, let the Holy Spirit guide you in what you ask. But sometimes you ask and do not receive. Why?

Principle # 3: Do Not Ask With A Wrong Motive

Sometimes you wonder why you have repeatedly asked God for something, and you have waited for a long time and did not receive the thing you asked for. James 4:3 gives us the answer,

> **You do not have, because you do not ask God. When you ask, you do not receive, because you ask with wrong motives, that you may spend what you get on your pleasures.**

You must understand that God owns everything you possess. He is the one who gave you everything you have. There is nothing you own that God did not give you. And that is the reason you must ask Him for everything. But the problem is, when you ask, you do not receive because you ask with a wrong motive. If you know that God gave you everything you own, why ask Him with a wrong motive?

The answer is simple: your motive is to spend or lavish what you are asking for on your selfish pleasures. You don't care about others. You care about your interest all the time You are not asking to receive so you can help others. You are not asking to praise and glorify God. The Greek word that is used in the text, "aiteo," means, "ask to be given." But the consequence for asking with a wrong motive is that you do not receive anything. Sometimes God allows you to get what you selfishly asked, for but that comes with a serious spiritual consequence. Why?

Principle # 4: Do Not Ask Stubbornly

When God allows you to get your way, serious consequences occur because you are more concerned about yourself than giving God glory. Instead of growing spiritually, you become a spiritual dwarf. How does this happen?

The way God dealt with stubborn asking was in the account of the children of Israel in Psalm 106:12-19,

Then they believed his promise and sang his praise, but they soon forgot what he had done and did not wait for his counsel. In the desert, they gave in to their craving; in the wasteland, they put

God to the test. So he gave them what they asked for, but sent a wasting disease upon them.

The consequence of stubborn asking can be very devastating. This passage refers to the stubborn attitude the children of Israel displayed in their wilderness experience with God. The children of Israel had broken their relationship and fellowship with God. But as far as God was concerned, He had made a covenant with Abraham, Israel's father. Frequently, the children of Israel break fellowship with God. And this caused them to become unreasonable and impatient with what they asked from God.

Although the children of Israel believed God's promise and praised Him for it, they quickly forgot all the miracles God had performed in Egypt to bring them out of slavery. They praised God sporadically, but frequently rebelled against Him. When they asked God for favor, they were impatient. They wanted whatever they asked for now. They craved all kinds of things they had in Egypt. They were looking backwards instead of forward. They trivialized God's provision for them in the wilderness.

When God allowed them to break fellowship with Him because of their stubborn asking, He also allowed them to suffer the consequence of rebellious asking. He gave them what they asked for, but also sent a wasting disease that ravaged them physically and spiritually. Instead of being spiritual giants for God, they became spiritual dwarfs.

Stubborn asking can drain your physical and spiritual energy. In many ways, we are like the children of Israel in the desert. Sometimes while we are in our spiritual desert, God allows us to experience the kind of training and discipline that we may not have gotten in any other way. We must also realize that unless we repent and return to the Lord so He can restore us to wholeness, refresh and revive us with His Spirit, we may stay in our desert for a long, lingering time. Stubborn asking is not good for you. What else do you need to learn about asking? Let us go to the reasons why we need to remain in Him.

Principle # 5: Remain In Him To Bear Fruit

While stubborn asking is not good for you, remaining in Him will bring a blessing to you. This is why remaining in Him requires you to stay in close relationship and fellowship with God in His Word, so you can bear much fruit. John 15:6-8, reads,

> **If anyone does not remain in me, he is like a branch that is thrown away and withers, such branches are picked up and thrown into the fire and burned. If you remain in me and my Word remains in you, ask whatever you wish and it will be given to you. This is to my Father's glory that you bear much fruit, showing yourselves to be my disciples.**

Earlier in John chapter 15, Jesus used the analogy of the vine tree, the gardener, and the branches to teach us a spiritual principle about the significance and blessings of remaining in the vine. Jesus identified Himself as the vine, God as the gardener, and born again believers as the branches.

I am the vine, and my Father is the gardener He cuts off every branch in me that bears no fruit, while every branch that does bear fruit, he prunes so that it will be even more fruitful. You are already clean because of the word I have spoken to you. Remain in me and I will remain in you. No branch can bear fruit by itself, it must remain in the vine. Neither can you bear fruit unless you remain in me. (John 15:1-4)

In this context, Jesus teaches that the only way we can be fruitful is that we must make a commitment to remain in Him. And as long as we remain in Him, God will continue to prune, nurture, and groom us, so we can continue to produce more fruit. In other words, only the branches that remain in the vine have the advantage of being pruned and the capacity of producing more fruit. In contrast, those branches that are dead are cut off and thrown away and burned in fire. When something is dead, it is put away. It serves no good purpose. It is just simply dead.

Principle # 6: Learn How to Bear Fruit

How do you bear fruit? You can share the gospel of Jesus Christ with somebody. You can give money for the gospel. You can go to a mission field, you can pray, you can help the needy, the poor, the disadvantaged, widow, and orphan, you can show love to people, you can sing, you can praise and worship God, you can start a ministry, etc., and there is no limit to what you can do to bear much fruit, as long as you remain in the vine.

One more thing: God is glorified when you bear much fruit. Bearing much fruit confirms that you are Jesus' disciples. Every time you bear much fruit, God is glorified. Bearing much fruit is not about you, it is about the Father's glory.

Principle # 7: Remain In His Word

To remain in Jesus means that we must commit to diligently study His Word. Unless you have a personal fellowship with Him in His Word, it will be impossible for us to bear fruit. To remain in Him prepares us to study His Word, memorize it, recall it and use it when we pray. Why?

First, God engrafted us into His Son, in whom we are to remain. By doing this, God established a new relationship between Him and us. However, in order for us to continue to enjoy this new relationship, Jesus demands that we must remain in His Word. To become fruitful and productive in this new life, we must remain effectively in Him. We must also let His Word remain effectively in us. Our growth in Him is based on our knowledge of His Word. His Word cannot remain in us if we do not diligently study it.

Second, if His Word effectively remains in us, we will be able to use it to defend and defeat the enemy when we pray in the same way Jesus used His Word to defeat the devil during His desert temptation experience in Matthew 4:1-11. Jesus was able to defeat the devil because He had abundant knowledge of God's Word in Him. During the temptation encounter, the devil challenged Jesus' authority three times, and Jesus used the Word of God to repel the devil's lies. Each time Jesus responded, "It is written," "It is written," "It is written." If the Word of God did not remain effectively in the Lord, He would not have been able to defeat the devil. And this is the reason you must diligently study the Word and let it remain in you, so that when you get into your desert experience, you will be able to say as the Lord did, "It is written." And there is more to learn about "remain."

Principle # 8: Remain In Wholesome Asking.

You have committed to remain in Him and His Word to remain in you, but how does this impact on your prayer and what you ask from God? Jesus teaches that to ask for anything from Him requires an "If - then" condition that will qualify you to ask Him for anything. And that condition is this, **"If you remain in me and my Words remain in you, ask whatever you wish and it will be given to you."** If you ask Jesus to do what you wish, then you must remain in Him and His Words must remain in you. Jesus made it clear that unless you remain in Him and His Words remains in you, you might as well not ask for anything you wish, because it will not be given to you. The condition for receiving what you wish is that you must remain in Him and His Words in you. Read the Word, study it, memorize it, use it, and let the Holy Spirit the teacher guide you to understand it.

Principle # 9: Ask In Confidence

The Apostle John teaches us another important lesson why we must ask in confidence. The word "confidence" means trust, and assurance in what you believe in. To ask in confidence requires that we ask without a doubt, based on the evidence we have.

I John 5:14-16, reads,

This is the confidence we have in approaching God, that if we ask anything according to his will, he hears us. And if we know that he hears us — whatever we ask — we know that we have what we asked of him.

In this context, the only requirement we have to comply with is that we must ask according to the will of God. We must be convinced without a doubt that we have the confidence that God hears us when we ask Him for anything. The knowledge that He hears us is confirmed in our hearts.

Also, our knowledge and the confidence we have in Him will enable us to ask according to His will. When we ask according to His will, we are convinced that God will honor our request. And we know that we are asking according to God's will if whatever we ask for will glorify Him. In other words, when we ask according to God's will, we eliminate selfish interests from our asking. We cannot ask according to God's will and doubt at the same time, because confidence and doubt are mutually exclusive. But our confidence is strengthened when we ask in the name of Jesus. Why?

Principle # 10: Ask In The Name Of Jesus

The ultimate teaching on asking and receiving is that every prayer must be sealed in the name of Jesus Christ. This is the "sine qua non" of all asking. No prayer is complete, without the name of Jesus. Why? The name of Jesus shatters and demolishes all devilish and demonic forces on earth. The name of Jesus is above all other names. The name of Jesus is sacred, holy and powerful. The name of Jesus breaks every yoke. The enemy shudders at the name of Jesus. All demonic strongholds are destroyed in the name of Jesus.

The Lord Jesus gave us specific instruction and direction on how to ask for all things to be done in His name. John 14:13-14, reads, "And I will do whatever you ask in my name, so that the Son may bring glory to the Father. You may ask me for anything in my name, and I will do it."

In this scripture, Jesus placed Himself as the only and final executor of all prayer requests. He promised us that He will do whatever we asked Him to do for us. But His promise will be executed on the condition that we ask in His name. And the reason for asking in His name is that His Father may be glorified in the Son. God testified that only in Jesus did He have a Son in whom He (God) was abundantly pleased.

At the mountain of transfiguration, God confirmed the Father-Son relationship and fellowship. Matthew 17:5 reads,

While he (Peter) was still speaking, a bright cloud enveloped them, and a voice from the cloud said, this is my Son, whom I love, with whom I am well pleased. Listen to him.

This relationship and fellowship between Jesus and His Father established for all time that Jesus is the only Son who pleases Him all the time, through all eternity. God commanded us to listen to Jesus through whom all our requests will be met, because He pleases, glorifies and does His will forever. And when you ask Him for anything, seal that prayer in the name of Jesus Christ our Lord. And God will execute whatever we ask for in the name of Jesus.

Questions for Reflection

Instruction: Respond with insight on asking and receiving.

1. Why should we ask God for anything?

   _____

   _____

   _____

   _____

2. How would the principles of asking help you in your prayer life?

   _____

   _____

   _____

   _____

3. Why ask for something over and over again?

   _____

   _____

   _____

   _____

4. Why should every prayer be sealed in the name of Jesus?

_____

_____

_____

_____

5. Would you be willing to discuss asking and receiving with friends at church?

_____

_____

_____

_____

Chapter Six

Pray With Self-Discipline

Everyone who competes in the games goes into strict training. They do it to get a crown that will not last; but we do it to get a crown that will last for ever.
(I Corinthians 9:25)

Self-discipline ought to play a major role in how you value your prayer life. Contrary to what some people may believe or say about praying, the fact is that effective prayer cannot be done at random.

If you are to be successful in your prayer life, you must incorporate self-discipline into it, because undisciplined life results into instability, inconsistency, inefficiency, lack of focus, confusion and failure.

The case for self-discipline can be made in every area of your life. It does not matter whether it is undisciplined eating, playing, sleeping, athletics, work, recreation, or undisciplined sexual behavior, you must make the hard choice to confront and deal with it.

Self-discipline is about setting up guidelines and rules of engagement that are necessary to enable you take control of the areas in your prayer life. One of the areas you need self-discipline is in time discipline.

Time Discipline

In a world that is in a flux, very fast-paced, with frequent changes in our work, recreation, and sleep schedules, we are hard pressed to set up a stable and consistent praying time. We often use this lack of time as our dominant excuse for not having a consistent praying time.

Sometimes we allow the enemy to clutter our time with other activities. We spend enormous hours watching television and rented movies early in the morning, we play PLAYSTATION, computer games and surf the Internet for all kinds of junk late at night. We engage in compulsive shopping and other mundane activities all day long.

Sometimes the drive for personal pleasures and other forms of indulgences distract us from having a disciplined prayer life. After we spend all week on our gig, we go to our one convenient service on Sunday morning to get our so-called prayer and praise groove on. And that's it. We have no prayer or Bible study time at home because our 24-hour-day has already been cluttered by the devil. Then we think the only prayer we need is the Pastor's altar call or the deacon's prayer, or the minister's prayer. Yes, all that is good, but it is not enough. You must study the Bible yourself and you must pray for yourself. You can't pray if you have not set the time and discipline yourself to do it.

Quality Time in Prayer

The value of spending quality time in prayer cannot be underestimated. When you pray, you must understand that you are encountering God in an intimate and personal fellowship that requires you to spend quality time with Him. When your prayer fellowship with God rank very high in your hierarchy of values, you must assign valuable time to it. You must also nurture that time until it becomes an essential part of your disciplined routine for daily living. The more highly you value that fellowship time, the more openly, frequently, and genuinely you will desire to spend that quality time alone with God. In other words, how important and intense your desire to engage God in your prayer time is, determines how you will respond to Him. But how much time is valuable quality time?

How Much Is Valuable Praying Time?

There are different opinions on whether you must pray daily or not. And while some people teach that daily prayer is not necessary so long as you pray only when you feel like praying, others teach that daily prayer is essential, but you must not feel obligated to it. Still others suggest that you try to make it as frequent as possible. But my personal opinion is that prayer fellowship with God is an imperative, which requires a daily commitment to prayer. But this does not mean that you lock yourself in a time that is inflexible. How much time you spend during one prayer session is a decision you and the Holy Spirit have to make together. Here is how you can evaluate yourself.

Praying Time Self-Evaluation

You can use this simple guide to calculate how much time you spend praying per week and how much time you spend in other activities per week.

There are seven days in a week, 24 hours a day. If you multiply seven days by 24 hours, you have 168 hours a week. And with these numbers, you can figure out how your weekly activity hours are distributed.

Example: 7 days x 24 hours = 168 hours

Average Weekly Activity Hours Distribution

Activity: Days/Hours Estimated Time
                              Per Week

Work at your job: 5 x 8 = 40
Drive to and from work: 5 x 2 = 10
Study: 7 x 1 = 7
Leisure (TV, Movies):   7 x 6 = 42
Shopping: 3 x 3 = 9
Housework: 7 x 1 = 7
Sleep: 7 x 7 = 49

Total: 164

This distribution shows that you spend 164 hours of the week in your different activities, and if you subtract this number from a total 168 hours you have in a week, what is left is four hours.

Example: Subtract 164 hours from 168 = 4 hours:

Let us assume that the leftover four hours a week is for prayer. How much of that time do you actually pray? Check it out.

Prayer Time Distribution: Available Weekly
Prayer Time = 4 hours

Minutes of Daily Prayer Per Week		Total Actual Prayer Minutes Per Week
Minutes	Minutes	Hours
1 x 7	7	0
5 x 7	35	0
10 x 7	70	1:10
20 x 7	140	1:20
30 x 7	210	3:30
40 x 7	280	4:40
50 x 7	350	5:50
60 x 7	420	7:00

As shown in this format, if you prayed 30 minutes a day, you would have prayed, 210 minutes or 3.5 hours a week. That is a little less than the four hours you have left in a week after you have used all your other weekly hours and times for your activities. If you prayed only five minutes a day, you would have spent 35 minutes a week in prayer. With these numbers, you can evaluate for yourself how much time you spend in prayer per week. As you look at these numbers, are you prepared to challenge, commit, and discipline yourself in order to maximize the time you spend alone with God? You must remember that how important and intense your desire to pray determines how you respond to God when you engage in that fellowship time with Him. The higher you place prayer in your hierarchy of activities, the higher the value you assign to it.

If you do not place the highest value on studying the Word of God and prayer, it does not matter how long you have been a Christian, you will be living a stunted Christian life. And you can think all you want about prayer, but that does not mean you have prayed. You can feel all you want about prayer, but that does not mean you have prayed. You can talk all you want about prayer, but that does not mean you have prayed. You can rationalize and argue all you want about prayer, but that does not mean you have prayed. Praying is an activity you must do. And when you do it, you will receive the blessing that come with it. Stop speculating about prayer and stop procrastinating to pray. Discipline yourself, commit to it and just do it. Pray not just for yourself, pray for others, too. That is the value of self-discipline in prayer. In case you may be wondering about the routine of prayer, good. You can build flexibility in your prayer, too. That is the next topic.

Questions for Reflection

Instruction: Respond to issues about discipline.

1. Why is self-discipline critical for a successful prayer life?

_____

_____

_____

2. Why is it important to have a designated time for prayer?

_____

_____

_____

3. Would you have a daily prayer time and stick with it? Why?

_____

_____

_____

4. What role should flexibility play in your prayer agenda?

__ __ __ __ __ __ __ __ __ __ __ __ __ __ __ __ __ __ __

__ __ __ __ __ __ __ __ __ __ __ __ __ __ __ __ __ __ __

__ __ __ __ __ __ __ __ __ __ __ __ __ __ __ __ __ __ __

5. How long should one prayer session last?

__ __ __ __ __ __ __ __ __ __ __ __ __ __ __ __ __ __ __

__ __ __ __ __ __ __ __ __ __ __ __ __ __ __ __ __ __ __

__ __ __ __ __ __ __ __ __ __ __ __ __ __ __ __ __ __ __

6. Would you be willing to share the values of discipline in prayer? Why?

__ __ __ __ __ __ __ __ __ __ __ __ __ __ __ __ __ __ __

__ __ __ __ __ __ __ __ __ __ __ __ __ __ __ __ __ __ __

__ __ __ __ __ __ __ __ __ __ __ __ __ __ __ __ __ __ __

Chapter Seven

Prayer Needs Planning

But I call to God and the Lord saves me. Evening, morning and noon I cry out in distress and he hears my voice.
(Psalm 55:16-17)

If we are to maintain an effective prayer life, then we must incorporate flexibility into it. Sometimes in an effort to establish regularity and consistency, we lock ourselves in such rigid schedules that flexibility becomes impossible. An inflexible prayer schedule can put enormous stress on our prayer life. Sometimes it can be so pressured that we begin to lose interest and our enthusiasm begins to decline, and consequently, our prayer life is tuned out.

However, providing flexibility and variety does not mean we are to sacrifice consistency. In other words, flexibility, variety, and regularity have to be balanced in order to give us the maximum benefit we need in our prayer life. By His own examples, the Lord Jesus teaches us three different ways we can use flexibility in our prayer. The first is flexibility in choice of prayer times. The second is flexibility in our choice of praying places, and the third is flexibility in our choice of prayer agenda.

Flexibility in Choosing Praying Time

Although the Lord Jesus stressed the importance of private prayer and the need to spend time alone with God, He was flexible in choosing His prayer times. He made full and effective use of the day. Sometimes He prayed early in the morning, sometimes during the day, sometimes in the evening and sometimes at night. He did not lock Himself in only one part of the day. And He did not compromise taking that time alone with His Father. When it was time to pray, He moved away from the crowds and the disciples He was training to a solitary place to pray. He chose a convenient time and made the best use of the time. Let's look at His examples.

Bible References	**Praying Times**
Mark 1:35, "Very early in the morning, while it was still dark, Jesus got up, left the house and went off to a solitary place, where he prayed."	Early Morning
Luke 4:42, "At daybreak, Jesus went out to a solitary place."	Morning
Luke, 3:21, "When all the people were being baptized, Jesus was baptized too. And as he was praying heaven was opened ..." (see John, 17, the Priestly prayer)	Day
Matthew 14:23, "After he had dismissed them, he went up on a mountainside by himself to pray. When evening came, he was there alone."	Evening
Luke 5:16, "But Jesus often withdrew to lonely places and prayed."	Evening

Matthew 26:36," Then Jesus went with his disciples to a place called Gethsemane, and he said to them, "Sit here, while I go over there and pray." (see Mark 14:32; Luke 22:41)	Night
Luke, 6:12, "One of those days, Jesus went out to the mountainside to pray and spent the night praying to God."	Night

While Jesus' examples of flexibility in choice of prayer times can help us to understand how we also can be flexible in choosing our prayer time, we can learn more examples from the Psalms.

Bible References	**Praying Times**
Psalm 5:3, "In the morning you hear my voice, O Lord, in the morning, I lay my requests before you and wait with expectation."	Morning
Psalm 88:13, "…But I cry to you for help, O Lord, in the morning my prayer comes before you."	Morning

Psalm 88:9, "I call to you O Lord every day, I spread out my hands to you."	Daily
Psalm 145:2, "Every day, I will praise you and extol your name for ever and ever."	Daily
Psalm 55:16-17, "But I call to God and the Lord saves me, evening, morning and noon. I cry out in distress and he hears my voice."	Evening Morning Noon
Psalm 77:2, "When I was in distress, I sought the Lord at night, I stretched my hands, and my soul refused to be comforted."	Night
Psalm 119:62, "At midnight, I rise to give you thanks for your righteous laws."	Midnight

While prayer does not always necessarily have to be in the morning, it is, however, important that you begin each day with prayer. There is something unique, refreshing and reassuring about having an early morning prayer time alone with God. However, to avoid being burdened by choosing only one part of the day, you must endeavor to schedule your prayer time during any part of the day, evening or night that is most convenient for you. Do not be afraid to make adjustments to your time when necessary.

But whatever you do, make sure that when that prayer times comes, you pray. How much time you should spend praying per session is a decision you and the Holy Spirit have to make together. Remember that this solitary time is a special time when you can express all your emotions, your crying, laughing, your worship, your praise, your weaknesses, your strengths, your frustrations, your hopes, your confidence, your trust and above all your faith and love to Him. Now, let us move on to flexibility in choice of praying places.

Flexibility In Choosing Praying Places

Although most of Jesus' recorded prayer places were outside the house or home, He provided clear guidelines on how prayer ought to be conducted in the home. We will get to this topic in another chapter. But for now, we shall concentrate on the uniqueness of Jesus' choice of praying places and how these apply to us.

Jesus was flexible in His choice of praying places even though He more frequently chose the mountains. He also prayed sometimes in the desert. In spite of where He chose, He was alone with His Father. His examples left room for flexibility. Here are Jesus' places of prayer.

Bible References	**Prayer Places**
Matthew 14:23, "After he had dismissed them, he went up on a mountainside by himself to pray. When evening came, he was there alone." (see Mark 6:46; Luke 6:12; John 6:15)	Mountainside alone
Luke 5:16, "Jesus often withdrew to lonely places and prayed." (see Luke 9:18)	Desert (Lonely places)

Flexibility in choosing prayer places allows you to find a convenient place to spend valuable time alone with the Lord. Most people prefer to pray in their home, and that is ideal if you have control over noise or other environmental distractions. Whatever you do, ensure that you have a convenient place for you to share a wonderful time of fellowship and blessing alone with God. There is something special about meeting God at that solitary place. Next is flexibility in choosing prayer agenda.

Flexibility in Choosing Praying Agenda

After you have chosen your prayer time and place, then comes the fun part. What are you going to talk and pray about? An agenda provides you with bullet points that are so vital and necessary for a meeting. But an agenda is also what you are to resolve with the Holy Spirit. Before you engage in a prayer encounter, you must already have something in mind to discuss. While you have your talking points, make sure you make room for the Holy Spirit to share and guide you as you pray. Do not forget reading the Word of God before you pray. Be prepared to pray the Word when you begin your prayer. We shall discuss fully why the vital role of knowing the Word of God, and praying the Word is an invaluable asset for strengthening your prayer life.

Questions for Reflection

Instruction: React to the values of choosing praying places and prayer agenda.

1. Why is it important to choose praying places carefully?

_____

_____

_____

_____

2. What factors would you consider in setting a prayer agenda?

_____

_____

_____

_____

3. Would you be willing to plan a prayer meeting for a church group? How?

_____

_____

_____

_____

Chapter Eight

Prayer Is Not About Pride

**And when you pray, do not be like the hypocrites,
for they love to pray standing in the Synagogues
and on street corners to be seen by men. I tell you
the truth, they have received their reward in full.
(Matthew 6:5)**

Often we have misconceptions on protocols about
praying in public or in private. Sometimes we wonder
which one is better — private or public prayer. We wonder
which one gets us the publicity, notoriety and approval we
need from people, or which one gets us the best results we
need from the Lord. Well, Jesus clarified the issues for us
in a series of teaching protocols about how we ought not to
pray.

Protocol # One: The Hypocrite

We begin with the protocol about why we should not pray like the hypocrites. First, a hypocrite by Jesus' standard lives a deceptive and double life. A hypocrite is a liar who says one thing and does the opposite. He does not practice what he preaches. The hypocrites Jesus referred to in this passage were all into getting as much public notoriety as they could when they prayed. They were friends of the public domain. They loved to impress people when they prayed. They sought validation from people. They were flamboyant and loved every bit of it. When they prayed in church, they were very conspicuous. They were noticed. And they impressed and entertained the congregation. The only problem with this is that Jesus said they already have received their reward in full. There is nothing else to look forward to. God is out in their prayer and man is in. Beware of this kind of prayer, Jesus cautions us. Stay away from this kind of prayer. What is next?

Protocol # Two: The Self-Righteous

Jesus confronted the arrogant self-righteous prayer attitude with the parable of the Pharisee and the Tax Collector, in Luke 18:9-14,

To some who were confident of their own righteousness and looked down on everybody else, Jesus told this parable. Two men went into the temple to pray, one a Pharisee and the other a Tax collector. The Pharisee stood up and prayed about himself. God, I thank you that I am not like the other men – robbers, evildoers, adulterers, – or even like this tax collector. I fast twice a week and give a tenth of all I get.

But the Tax Collector stood at a distance. He would not even look up to heaven, but beat his heart and said, "God, have mercy on me a sinner." I tell you that this man rather than the other went home justified before God. For everyone who exalts himself will be humbled, and he who humbles himself will be exalted.

In this parable, two different attitudes to prayer are displayed. The Pharisee prayed the arrogant and self-righteous prayer and the Tax Collector prayed a humble prayer. Jesus clarified the difference between the Pharisee and the Tax Collector's praying attitudes.

The Pharisee

In Matthew chapter 23, Jesus defines the characteristics of the Pharisee. He called them teachers of the law and hypocrites who do not practice what they preach. (v.3). He called them blind guides who do everything for public display, acclaim and spectacle. They give their tithe but neglect justice, mercy and faithfulness. They are blind guides, full of greed and indulgence. They are whitewashed tombs, snakes and a brood of vipers. These are pretty profound and harsh characterization of the Pharisees. But Jesus knew them and defined them accurately. Wow.

The Tax Collector

Tax collectors were men who collected public taxes. They stayed in booths to collect money, tolls, and tributes for a city, state, or government in the ancient Roman Empire (much like the IRS today). Tax collectors had very poor reputations in community and society because they were corrupt from collecting excess money and pocketing some for themselves. They were dishonest public servants. While the Pharisees were extreme legalists, the tax collectors were extreme liberals. This is not a pretty picture either for the tax collectors.

The Similarity and the Difference

But both the Pharisee and the Tax Collector went to the temple to pray to God. The difference is their attitude to prayer and how they presented themselves.

Proud Attitude

The Pharisee's attitude was wrapped up in self-righteousness based on pride, arrogance, boastful, pompous, mean, talkative, criticism, tearing down others, gossip about others, legalism, perfect, flawless, faultless, without defect, having impressive and impeccable religious, professional and personal credentials. It's all about him. God was not the focus or center of his prayer.

The consequence of the Pharisee's prayer was very devastating. His pride and arrogance would not let him worship God. He went to the temple to showcase his credentials, his accomplishments, and self-righteousness. His arrogance would not let him seek God. As far as he was concerned, God had nothing to offer to him. He had no room for spiritual growth and no room for God to do something new in his life. His religious obligations were contained and enclosed in his prayer, except God. And because God was shut out of his prayer life, he lost everything. God did not pronounce him righteous. What a tragedy.

Humble Attitude

But for the Tax Collector, his attitude was wrapped up in confession and humility. He had no impressive credentials, no accomplishments to boast about, he spoke only few words from a broken and contrite heart. He came to the temple to confess and worship God. He recognized and acknowledged his sinfulness. He acknowledged that only God could forgive and show him mercy. He acknowledged that true worship humbles. In worship, he was forgiven, cleansed, purified, justified, healed, restored and made whole.

What a victory.

Practice Humility

The parable of the Pharisee and Tax Collector teaches us about humility. We must humble ourselves before God when we pray because the rewards are refreshing, beneficial and joyful. We must humble ourselves, because the Lord hates the proud and arrogant. When we humble ourselves, He will reward us and bless us. Matthew 23:12, reads, "For whoever exalts himself will be humbled and whoever humbles himself will be exalted." Also Proverbs 11:2, says, "When pride comes, then comes disgrace, but with humility comes wisdom." There are several other Bible passages that counsel us about the consequences of pride and arrogance. Proverbs 8:13, reads, "The fear of the Lord is to hate evil. I hate pride and arrogance, evil behavior and perverse speech." So when you pray, watch your attitude, your behavior, and your speech. Stay away from the Pharisee's arrogant attitude, but stick with the Tax Collector's humble attitude. Next topic will be the protocols of private prayer.

Questions for Reflection

Instruction: React to concerns about pride.

1. Why should prayer not be about personal pride?

_____

_____

_____

2. What is humility and why should we humble ourselves
   when we pray?

_____

_____

_____

3. Why did Jesus have a problem with self-righteous
   people?

_____

_____

_____

4. What kind of prayer attitude did the Pharisee and the Tax Collector show?

_____

_____

_____

5. How would you avoid pride and arrogance in your prayer?

_____

_____

_____

6. How would you demonstrate a humble attitude when you pray?

_____

_____

_____

Chapter Nine

Prayer: Time Alone With God

But when you pray, go into your room, close the door and pray to your Father, who is unseen. Then your Father, who sees what is done in secret, will reward you.
(Matthew, 6:6)

The need to spend valuable prayer time alone with God cannot be underestimated. Jesus took private prayer seriously. He taught it and practiced it. He gave specific instructions about how to pray in private. He also clarified for us the benefits of private prayer.

Reasons for Private Prayer Time

There are several reasons why we must pray in private.

- to avoid distractions, including physical, environmental, and mental distractions
- to give respect and honor to God, the Lord Jesus and the Holy Spirit
- to recognize God as the ultimate focus and center of our prayer
- to activate our access and freedom to meet with God alone
- to demonstrate the special nature of our relationship with Him
- to demonstrate in a most profound way, our absolute dependence on Him
- to express only those things that can be shared with Him in private
- to spend quality time alone with God
- to pray and rejoice in private with Him
- to share our vulnerability with God alone
- to seek spiritual power and strength from Him
- to receive direct instructions and guidance about being obedient and confident in Him and to express our feelings, thoughts, emotions and concerns
- to experience the freedom to fellowship with Him
- to express the freedom to praise and worship Him
- to keep open our heart, mind and ears to hear Him

And there are much more. But for now, we must move on to learn how Jesus practiced to pray in private, so that we can learn how to pray in private from Him.

Jesus' Private Prayers

Many times in the gospels, Jesus prayed in private alone and away from the very disciples He was training. Here are some examples: Matthew 14:23, "After he had dismissed them, he went up on a mountainside by himself to pray. When evening came, he was there alone." (see Mark 1:35; 6:45; 6:46; Luke 4:42; 5:16; 6:12; 9:18; 11:1-4; Matthew 26:36-44; Mark 14:32-39; Luke 22:41-42; John 6:15).

These passages that recorded Jesus' prayer alone with God validate the fact that Jesus considered private prayer very important. He prayed privately before and after His preaching, teaching, and healing ministries. The times He spent alone with God in prayer allowed Him to express those things that could only be shared in private.

Guidelines for Private Prayer

With His examples, Jesus gave us specific guidelines and protocols for spending time alone with God in prayer. Let us consider those guidelines from Matthew 6:6,

Guideline # 1: Pray In Secret

- Go into your room (private place)
- Close the door
- Pray to your Father who is unseen (in secret)
- Receive your reward

This guideline validates Jesus' emphasis on private prayer. In other words, only as you encounter God in your private time alone with Him will you be able to fully and intimately share in this special moment your deepest thoughts, emotions, desires, frustrations, hopes, trust, confidence, love and faith in His presence. Only during this private moment will you be able to hear Him, listen to His counsel as He responds to your petition or cry. When you have spent that time alone with God, you are ready to receive your rewards from Him. Remember, He is the giver of all good gifts and He strengthens and rewards those who seek Him diligently.

Notice, the phrase "when you pray, close your door," leaves room for the praying activity to take place either in the morning, afternoon, evening or night. But whatever time you choose to pray, you ought to make it a private time with God. You ought to cherish that solitary time alone with Him. And be prepared to obey and act on the counsel He gives you.

Guideline # 2: Do Not Repeat Meaningless Words

The challenge to be precise or specific with the words you use when you pray must be taken very seriously. Matthew 6:7-8, reads, **"And when you pray, do not keep on babbling like pagans, for they think they will be heard because of their many words. Do not be like them, for your Father knows what you need before you ask him"**

In this text, Jesus made it absolutely clear that you cannot repeat meaningless words like the pagans or those who do not know the Lord Jesus as their personal Savior. The reason some people repeat the same words over and over is because they have very limited knowledge of the Word of God. They spend little time studying the Word. Consequently, the less Word of God you know, the more likely you are to repeat the few you know. In contrast, the more Word of God you know, the more likely you will use more variety in your prayer to speak to your specific needs.

Also, because the pagans have erroneous knowledge of the Word of God, they think that God will hear them better if they repeated meaningless words. They fail to understand that God does not answer our prayer because of our abundant repetition of meaningless words. To avoid unnecessary repetition, you ought to study the Word of God and use it when you pray. The more the Word of God you pray, it will help you to eliminate meaningless repetition. Keep your prayer language precise and specific. God does not hear you just because you use many words. And since God knows your needs before you ask, it is not necessary to exaggerate what He already knows. Be specific in your asking. The next topic is persistence in prayer.

Questions for Reflection

Instruction: Respond to matters of private prayer.

1. What are the reasons for having a private praying time alone with God?

   _____

   _____

   _____

2. How does having prayer guidelines enhance your prayer life?

   _____

   _____

   _____

3. Why should you not repeat meaningless words when you pray?

   _____

   _____

   _____

4. Why should your prayer not be about impressing people in public?

_____

_____

_____

5. Why did Jesus teach the value of praying in secret?

_____

_____

_____

6. Would you be willing to lead prayer meetings on private prayer? Why?

_____

_____

_____

Chapter Ten

Pray and Don't Give Up

Then Jesus told his disciples a parable to show them that they should always pray and not give up.
(Luke, 18:1)

Sometimes you are concerned about how long you are to pray about a particular thing. If you prayed about something, once, twice, three times or even more, how do you know when to stop praying? Jesus answered this question by teaching His disciples that they should never quit, stop asking or praying until God answers.

This response is clarified in the parable of the widow in Luke 18:1-8. In the parable, Jesus said, "In a certain town there was a judge who neither feared God nor cared about men. And there was a widow in that town, who kept coming to him with a plea, "Grant me justice against my adversary." For sometime he refused. But finally, he said to himself, "Even though I don't fear God or care about men, yet because this widow keeps bothering me, I will see that she gets justice, so that she won't eventually wear me out with her coming." And the Lord said, "Listen to what the unjust judge says. And will not God bring about justice for his chosen ones, who cry out to him day and night. Will he keep putting them off?" I tell you, he will see that they get justice."

The Imperative to Persist In Prayer

In this parable, Jesus emphasized that it is imperative to persist in prayer until you get a response from God. It does not matter how long you have been praying about something. And so long as the problem or need is not resolved, the need to continue praying will persist. In other words, you are to continue to pray for that specific need until you are sure the answer has been given.

Furthermore, you must understand that persevering in prayer has a lingering effect. But the lingering time must serve as your motivation to continue praying. And so long as the enemy, the problem, or the disturbing condition remains, you must not quit praying.

Because the potential to get easily discouraged when you do not receive immediate answers to your prayer escalates. Jesus counsels you to remain steadfast. Why? Because the judge (**the antagonist**) was so proud, and arrogant, he deliberately refused to grant the widow justice. He is the instigator or motivator for the widow's persistence. If the instigator or antagonist was obstinate and stubborn, the need to continue praying remains.

Sometimes we are like the widow. The more we experience opposition and pressure, the more the urge to continue praying intensifies. However, you must understand that when one need is met, another emerges, and that is why Jesus encourages us to pray and not give up.

In this situation, we must understand that a delayed response is God's way of training us to learn how to trust Him. God always responds to our need speedily at His appointed time. In comparison, if the arrogant judge had sense enough after a prolonged appeal and pleading to grant the widow justice, how much more will a righteous God answer your prayer faster and on time, without excessive and indefinite delay.

Prayer in Warfare

You must be aware that persistence in prayer indicates that you are in warfare. You are in combat. And you must be dressed and armed with the Word of God, which is both your offensive and defensive weapon. Ephesians 6:10-18, reads, **"Finally, be strong in the Lord and his mighty power, put on the full armor of God so that you can take your**

stand against the devil's schemes. For our struggle is not against flesh and blood, but against the rulers, against the authorities, against the powers of this dark world, and against the spiritual forces of evil in the heavenly realms.

When you recognize that you are in warfare against these forces, the need to continue praying becomes more compelling. As the warfare and opposition intensifies, you must take hold of your combat weapon. Ephesians 6:13-18 provides you with the combat tools and protocols.

Combat Protocol # 1: Get Ready for Defense

- Put on your full armor of God (the Word of God)
- Stand your ground (prepare your defense position)
- Do everything to stand (clean your weapon, get your ammunition ready)
- Stand firm (secure you defensive line with the belt of truth, the Word)

Combat Protocol # 2: Get Ready for Offensive

- Wear your breastplate of righteousness
- Wear your boots (ready to launch an offensive with the Word)
- Protect yourself from enemy weapons of attack with your shield of faith

- Saturate your mind with the Word of God, your offensive weapon

Combat Protocol # 3: Then Launch Your Attack

- Pray in the Spirit at all times (indefinite attack, all occasions)
- Keep on praying. Don't give up. Never quit. (all kinds of prayer, you name it)

Finally, no matter how tough it gets, never quit praying. Stay until you get the answer from God. Be prepared to accept yes, no, or delay from God. And don't doubt God, because faith and doubt are mutually exclusive. He has the best for you.

Questions of Reflection

Instruction: React to the issues of prayer warfare.

1. Why do we recognize prayer as warfare?

_____

_____

_____

_____

2. What are the protocols for engaging in prayer warfare?

_____

_____

_____

_____

3. Why should we pray without giving up?

_____

_____

_____

_____

4. What are the weapons with which we fight the warfare?

_ _

_ _

_ _

_ _

5. Would you be willing to share your experiences with Christian warfare? Why?

_ _

_ _

_ _

_ _

Chapter Eleven

Know: The Word Factor

**For the Word of God is living and active. Sharper
than any double-edged sword, it penetrates, even
to dividing soul and spirit, joints and marrows; it
judges the thoughts and attitudes of the heart.
(Hebrews 4:12)**

Earlier in the previous chapters we talked about the
importance of prayer in our lives. We also discussed
the value of spending time alone with God and why we must
not give up praying. But what makes prayer effective is the
focus of this chapter.

Effective prayer is not determined by the amount of
words you can speak or your eloquence or how articulate
your language sounds. It is not determined by how impressive you come across to people. But effective prayer is the

work of the Holy Spirit, the power of the Word of God, and how you use the Word in your prayer.

To pray effectively, it is imperative that you know the Word of God. This means that you have to make a conscious and deliberate decision to study the Word of God. Here are the reasons.

1. The Word of God is the final authority that underscores and establishes our faith in God. The Word enables you to act in faith, because faith comes by hearing and hearing through the Word of God (Romans 10:17).

2. The Word of God is settled in heaven and on earth. It does not change. What it said yesterday, it says today and will say in the future It also endures throughout all eternity and generations (Psalm 119:89-92, "Your Word O Lord is eternal, it stands firm in the heavens. Your faithfulness continues throughout all generations, you established all the earth and it endures. The heavens and earth are established by the Word and we are to anchor our faith in the Lord through His Word.

3. You are mandated to let the Word of God remain (dwell) in you richly. Let the Word of Christ remain in you richly as you teach and admonish one another, with all wisdom, and as you sing psalms, hymns, and spiritual songs with gratitude in your hearts to God

(Colossians 3:17-18). In other words, as you teach, instruct, counsel and encourage others, it is imperative that you study the Word for yourself, memorize, meditate, internalize, visualize, and recall it so that your mind becomes a reservoir, you can draw abundantly from when you pray.

4. The Word of God purifies and cleanses you from sin. "How can a young man keep himself pure? By living according to your Word." (Psalm 119:9)

5. The Word acts as a deterrence from sin. When you hide the Word in your heart, it keeps you away from sinning. "I have hidden your Word in my heart that I might not sin against you." (Psalm 119:11)

6. The Word directs our footsteps and helps us walk away from sin. "Direct my footsteps according to your Word. Let no sin rule over me." (Psalm 119:133)

7. The Word is a lamp that shines and gives you light in the path you walk so you do not stumble and fall. "Your Word is a lamp to my feet and a light for my path." (Psalm 119:105)

8. The revealed Word gives you understanding. "The unfolding of your Word gives light, it gives understanding to the simple." (Psalm 119:30)

9. The Word judges your heart, conscience, and lays everything about you open. "For the Word of God is living and active, sharper than any double-edged sword, it penetrates even to dividing soul and spirit,

joints and marrow, it judges the thoughts and attitudes of the heart." (Hebrews 4:12)

10. The Word reveals and uncovers everything about you. "Nothing in all creation is hidden from God's sight everything is laid bare before the eyes of him, to whom we must give account." (Hebrews 4:13)

11. The Word is the sword of the Spirit and your offensive weapon for fighting the enemy.

12. The Word enables you to pray in the Spirit on all occasions. "Take the helmet of salvation, and the sword of the Spirit which is the Word of God. And pray in the Spirit on all occasions with all kinds of prayers and requests." (Ephesians 6:17-18)

13. The Word is flawless. "As for God, his way is perfect, the Word of the Lord is flawless." (it is without error) (II Samuel 22:31)

14. The Word burns like fire in your heart and in your bones. When the Word remains abundantly in your heart, it will burn like fire, enclosed in your bones. And you will desire to speak during prayer. You will be enthusiastic to share it with others. You cannot hold it in. Jeremiah cried out, "But if I say, I will not mention his name, his Word in my heart burns like a fire shut up in my bones. I am weary of holding it in. Indeed I cannot." (Jeremiah 20:9)

15. The Word is like a hammer that breaks a rock in pieces. "Is not my Word like fire," declared the Lord,

"and like a hammer that breaks a rock in pieces?" (Jeremiah 23:29)

These compelling reasons for knowing the Word of God are intended to help you understand the power of the Word when you use it to pray. In other words, the Word of God is our greatest weapon we have to fight the enemy when we get into prayer warfare.

Furthermore, you must make every endeavor to find delight and joy in your study of the Word. As Jeremiah did, "When your Words came, I ate them, they were my joy and my heart's delight, for I fear your name, O Lord, God Almighty" (Jeremiah 15:16)

Let us therefore eat the Word of God, because it is sweeter than honey. "How sweet are your Words to my taste, sweeter than honey to my mouth." If the Word of God is sweet in your mouth, then use it effectively when you pray to achieve the greatest results God has purposed for you as you spend that time alone with Him in prayer.

Questions for Reflection

Instruction: Respond with insight on the value of knowing God's Word.

1. Why is it imperative that we know the Word of God?

— —

— —

— —

2. What are the benefits of knowing the Word of God?

— —

— —

— —

3. What are the risks of not studying the Word of God?

— —

— —

— —

4. Why did Jesus teach that the Word of God must remain in us abundantly?

_____

_____

_____

5. Why should we read the Word of God with enthusiasm?

_____

_____

_____

6. Would you be willing to teach the value of knowing God's Word to a group? How?

_____

_____

_____

Chapter Twelve

Pray: The Word Factor

... So is my Word that goes out of my mouth. It will not return to me empty, but will accomplish what I desire, and achieve the purpose for which I sent it.
(Isaiah 55:10)

Your Power Is In The Word

In the preceding chapter we enumerated several reasons for knowing the Word of God. The focus of this chapter is on the imperative to use the Word of God when we pray. We must not underestimate the power of the spoken Word. There is no force more powerful than the Word of God. There are several reasons for us to understand the power of the Word of God when we pray.

Reason # 1: The Word brings what is spoken into existence

The Word of God has a creative power to bring what is spoken into existence. We can validate this statement with the fact that the universe God created, came to be by God's creative Word. Genesis 1:1-3, and 5, reads, "In the beginning God created the heavens and the earth. Now the earth was formless and empty, darkness was over the surface of the deep and the Spirit of God was hovering over the waters. And God said, "Let there be light" and "there was light..." "God called the light day." In His creative act, God completed in six days the creation of the heavens and the earth by His spoken Word. God said, and what He spoke came to be. We can also speak things into being.

Reason # 2: The Word produces positive results

We must recognize that God's creative Words produced good and positive results. "God saw all He had made and it was very good." (Genesis 1:31)

When God spoke, the Word accomplished the purpose for which it was spoken.

Reason # 3: Misused Word can produce negative results

Because the spoken word can be so powerful, we must be careful with how we use words and the kind of words we utter, even when we pray. In other words, we must learn how to speak positive words instead of negative words. When we speak positive words, we harvest positive results, and when we speak negative words, we also harvest negative results.

Reason # 4: Watch the tongue, it can spill life or death

If we are God's spokesperson, then we are to speak only worthy words and not worthless words. "If you utter worthy words and not worthless words, you will be my spokesman," declares the Lord (Jeremiah 15:19). We are also cautioned about how we use our tongue. We are to watch our tongue because the Bible says that "The tongue has the power of life and death. And those who love it will eat its fruits." (Proverbs 18:21). And the Bible also says that we shall be held accountable for every careless word we speak. Matthew 12:26 reads, "But I tell you that men will have to give account on the day of judgment for every careless word they have spoken." In other words, if we misuse or abuse the Word of God, then we will suffer the consequences. If we speak life, we harvest life, but if we speak death, we harvest death. So we are warned.

Since we have been warned about the power of the spoken word, and the power of the Word of God, we must be careful when we pray the Word, knowing that the Word of God has a profound impact on the outcome of our prayer.

Eight Reasons To Pray The Word Of God

First, praying the Word of God requires us to read, study the Word intensely, memorize, internalize, visualize, meditate, recall and use it during prayer. As we read the Word, we are listening to the Lord. In the process, the Holy Spirit helps us to understand the Word and enables us to speak it boldly when we pray. During prayer, we use the authority of the Word the Lord has deposited in us through the Holy Spirit, to declare God's power.

Second, we must recognize that the Lord has given us the keys to the Kingdom of Heaven and the Earth, and whatever we bind or lose on Earth will be bound or loosed in Heaven. (Matthew 16:19) What an awesome power and authority the Lord has given us. Let us use it with great care.

Third, we can use the authority of the Word of God as a hammer to break and demolish all obstacles, restrictions, brick walls, shackles, chains, and yokes that block our way. "Is not my Word like fire?" declares the Lord, "And like a hammer that breaks a rock in pieces?" If it is, then we must use it and declare it during prayer.

Fourth, we must use the authority of the Word to bind all demonic, natural, and supernatural forces warring against us. Ephesians 6:12, "For our struggle is not against flesh or blood, but against the rulers, against the authorities, against the powers of darkness of this dark world, and against the spiritual forces of evil in the heavenly realms." (see Matthew 16:19).

Fifth, we can use the Word of God to bind selfish forces, and evil spirits that hold us hostage — such as, the spirit of pride, arrogance, envy, greed, lust, jealousy, anger, hatred, coveting, lying, cheating, gossip, slander, indulgence, over-eating, gluttony, idolatry, adultery, fornication, division, indiscipline, selfish ambition, cursing, dirty language, rebellion, witchcraft, mind control, domination, manipulation, deceit, complaint, argumentation, nagging, drunkenness, grumbling, blaming, negativism, disobedience, etc. We can overcome these negative forces when we declare the authority of the Word of God.

Sixth, we can use the power of the Word of God to declare healing on the sick and set people free from all kinds of diseases. Isaiah 53:3, "But he was pierced for our transgressions, he was crushed for our iniquities, the punishment that brought us peace, was upon him, and by his wounds, we are healed." (see I Peter 2:24). Also, the Lord promised that He will not bring any of the Egyptians' diseases on us if we obeyed His Word. In Exodus 15:26, "The Lord said, If you listen carefully to the voice of the Lord your God, and do what is right in his eyes, if you pay attention to his commands, and keep all his decrees, I will not bring on you any of the diseases I brought on the Egyptians, for I am the Lord who heals you." What a wonderful promise.

The Lord's promises of healing continued in Exodus 25:16, "I will take away sicknesses from among you and none will miscarry, or be barren in your land, I will give you a full life span." Also in Psalm 103:3, "The Lord forgives all our sins, and heals our diseases." The Lord has made his healing promises to us and it is up to us to receive and act on them by faith.

Seventh, we can use the Word to declare affirmations of love, grace, peace, joy, health, wealth, riches, success, victory, wisdom, power, mercy, understanding, forgiveness, caring, compassion, giving, helps, comfort, wholeness, holiness, courage, truth, excellence, progress, faith, confidence, trust, integrity, honesty, character, and hope. Philippians 4:9, "Finally, brothers, whatever is right, whatever is true, whatever is pure, whatever is lovely, whatever is admirable, if anything is excellent, think about such things." When you declare affirmations in your prayer, you will experience positive, miraculous results. Speak life instead of death.

Eight, we can use the authority of the Word of God to rebuke and resist the devil's erroneous use of the Word of God to entrap us to sin. I Peter 5:9 reads, "Be self-controlled and alert. Your enemy the devil prowls around like a roaring lion, looking for someone to devour. Resist him, standing firm in faith, because you know that your brothers throughout the world are undergoing the same kind of sufferings."

Furthermore, we are commanded to resist the devil and he will flee from us. He will run away. James 4:7, "Submit yourselves then to God. Resist the devil and he will flee from you..." But how do we resist the devil?

How To Resist The Devil

Jesus taught us how to resist the devil with His encounter with the devil in the desert, after He had fasted forty days and forty nights and was hungry in Matthew, 4:1-11, "Then Jesus was led by the Spirit into the desert to be tempted by the devil."

At this encounter, the devil came to Jesus and challenged Jesus' authority, His Sonship and His integrity. This is how it happened.

Scene One: "Then Jesus was led by the Spirit into the desert to be tempted by the devil." (v.1)

Challenge # 1: The tempter came to him and said, "If you are the Son of God, tell these stones to become bread." (v. 3)

Response and Resistance # 1: Jesus answered, "It is written, 'Man does not live on bread alone, but on every Word that comes from the mouth of God.'" (v.4)

Scene Two: "Then the devil took him to the holy city and had him stand on the highest point of the temple." (v. 5)

Challenge # 2: "If you are the Son of God," he said, "throw yourself down. For it is written, he will command his angels concerning you and they will lift you up in their hands so that you will not strike your foot against a stone." (v.6)

Response and Resistance # 2: Jesus answered him, "It is written, Do not put the Lord your God to the test." (v. 7)

Scene Three: "Again the devil took him to a very high mountain and showed him all the kingdoms of the world and their splendor." (v.6)

Challenge # 3: "All this I will give you," he said, "If you will bow down and worship me." (v.7)

Response and Resistance # 3: Jesus said to him, "Away from me, Satan, For it is written, 'Worship the Lord your God, and serve him only.'" (v.10)

The Finale: "The devil shamefully flew away from Jesus and the angels attended him." (v.11)

Speak The Word

During Jesus' encounter with the devil, the Word of God was the greatest weapon Jesus used to resist and defeat the devil, his craftiness, tricks and deception. The Word repels his plans. And this is the profound reason we must read the Word, memorize, internalize, saturate our minds with it, recall and use it as our offensive and defensive weapon to resist all demonic attacks and tricks daily.

When you pray, you must be sure to speak the Word with authority, power, faith and confidence. The Word will perform and fulfill the purpose for which God has sent it. It will not return to him empty. Resist the devil with the Word, and he will shamefully flee far away from you. Your power is in the Word. Speak the Word.

Questions for Reflection

Instruction: React with insight to praying the Word.

1. Why is it imperative to pray the Word of God?

   __ __ __ __ __ __ __ __ __ __ __ __ __ __ __

   __ __ __ __ __ __ __ __ __ __ __ __ __ __ __

   __ __ __ __ __ __ __ __ __ __ __ __ __ __ __

2. Why is your praying power in the Word of God?

   __ __ __ __ __ __ __ __ __ __ __ __ __ __ __

   __ __ __ __ __ __ __ __ __ __ __ __ __ __ __

   __ __ __ __ __ __ __ __ __ __ __ __ __ __ __

3. What weapons do we use to resist the devil?

   __ __ __ __ __ __ __ __ __ __ __ __ __ __ __

   __ __ __ __ __ __ __ __ __ __ __ __ __ __ __

   __ __ __ __ __ __ __ __ __ __ __ __ __ __ __

4. What would happen if you prayed without the Word of God?

   __ __ __ __ __ __ __ __ __ __ __ __ __ __ __

   __ __ __ __ __ __ __ __ __ __ __ __ __ __ __

   __ __ __ __ __ __ __ __ __ __ __ __ __ __ __

5. Could you pray the Word when you are not speaking it audibly? How?

_____

_____

_____

6. Explain the consequences of not praying the Word?

_____

_____

_____

Chapter Thirteen

Pray: The Fear Factor

I sought the Lord, and he answered me, he delivered me from all my fears.
(Psalm 34:4)

Now, you have learned how to defeat the devil with the Word of God. The next challenge is how to defeat fear. Fear is the next enemy you must defeat. But first, we must consider different kinds of fear, what causes fear and what we can do to defeat it. In focus here are three kinds of fear: natural fear, negative fear and positive fear.

Natural Fear

Fear is natural and real and its impact can be devastating. Fear is insidious because it feeds on itself. Fear creates a vicious cycle. According to Kriegel and Patler, sometimes "fear is self-fulfilling, self-perpetuating, and self-reinforcing. Once underway, it gathers its own head of steam like snow ball rolling down hill."

Fear also operates in cycles, which sometimes is paralyzing. Kriegel and Patler noted that "fear cycle, begins with the imagination running wild, making everything seem worse than it is and magnifying the possible consequence of failing until they experience the horrible and catastrophic dimensions." They also observed that fear eats confidence and self-esteem. It eats into your own pride and self esteem. And when you are caught in the fear cycle, the consequences become horrific. Sometimes you think your life is falling apart.

Fear distorts perception. You see what you believe. You exaggerate your perceived difficulty. Everything becomes difficult. Everywhere you look, you see obstacles that will make it impossible for you to achieve anything. Fear can be sneaky. Often you are not aware of it. Consequently, you may not understand how your mind is exaggerating, making everything seem more difficult and debilitating.

Typically, you respond to fear with freezing or panic, either to slow down or speed up, overreact or under-react. You jam on the brakes or flood it. Sometimes fear stops you dead. In the freeze mode, you procrastinate, and avoid what seems to be frightening you. But when you are in the panic mode, you speed up. You don't communicate well, concentrate or think clearly. You act without thinking. And once your fear has been confirmed, self-incrimination begins. Tragically, when you are afraid, your performance does not reflect your real ability.

Negative Fear

Negative fear is similar to natural fear, with very little variations. Negative fear comes from the devil, and it can also have a very devastating and paralyzing impact on your life. Sometimes its impact can be so overwhelming, it may result in all sorts of negative physical, social, emotional, and psychological problems.

Negative fear may result in depression, self-isolation, inactivity, low self-image, low self-esteem, inability to perform, self-pity, lack of ambition, and inability to take personal responsibility. It incapacitates, and reinforces dependency behavior. It is the weapon the devil uses to hinder people from achieving their life goals.

Negative fear casts doubt on everything God has purposed for you. It reinforces negative imaginations in your mind, prompting negative mental images, which clutter your mind. It manifests itself in dominant ways, such as fear of death, fear of the devil, fear of failure, fear of disease and sickness, fear of making mistakes, fear of rejection and ridicule, fear of taking risks, fear of loneliness, fear of danger, fear of darkness,. It breeds anxiety, stress, fear of abandonment, fear of exploitation, fear of physical and emotional hurt, fear of loosing your job, fear of poverty, fear of debt, fear of people in powerful positions, fear of the unknown, etc.

Confronting Negative Fear

As real as natural and negative fear manifestations may be, you must understand that God has given you His Word as a weapon to overcome the constraints of natural and negative fear. And you must use it. In Psalm 34:4, we read, "I sought the Lord and he answered me, he delivered me from all my fears." This scripture declared that when you seek the Lord in all circumstances, conditions and situations, He will deliver you from all your fears, without exception. And you must believe it by faith. All means capital ALL.

Next, Psalm 23:4, confirms that God delivers you from your fear, "Even though I walk through the valley of the shadow of death, I will fear no evil, for you are with me, your rod and your staff, they comfort me." Furthermore, Psalm 56:3, reads, "When I am afraid, I will trust in you, in God whose Word I praise. In God I trust, I will not be afraid, what can mortal man do to me?" Your trust in God and your confidence in His Word are your weapons for defeating negative fear. And you still have to deal with positive fear.

Benefits of Positive Fear

Since we can defeat negative fear with the Word of God, we can also benefit from positive fear with the Word of God. But first, we need to answer the question: What is positive fear? Positive fear is from God. It is fear you experience out of reverence to God as He expresses His love to you. It is the fear that requires you to respond to God in obedience to His Word and commands. It is your response to God's awesomeness, holiness, and sovereignty over your life.

Positive fear requires that you are only to fear the Lord and nothing else and no one else in heaven and on earth. Isaiah 8:3, reads, "The Lord Almighty is the one you are to regard as holy, he is the one you are to fear, he is the one you are to dread."

The Bible has innumerable benefits of positive fear. And here are some of them.

Benefit # 1: Positive fear enables you to experience the awesomeness of God and keeps you from sinning against Him

After God had given the Ten Commandments to the children of Israel through Moses, the people trembled with fear. Exodus 20:19-20 reads, "When the people saw the thunder, and lightening, and heard the trumpets, and saw the mountain in smoke, they trembled with fear. They stayed at a distance, and said to Moses, "Speak to us yourself and we will listen. But do not have God speak to us or we will die." Moses said to the people, "Do not be afraid, God has come to test you, to see that the fear of God will be with you, to keep you from sinning." Awesome.

Benefit # 2: The fear of the Lord is the beginning of understanding

If you seek wisdom, you will find it in the fear of the Lord. Psalm 111:10, reads, "The fear of the Lord is the beginning of wisdom and all who follow his precepts have good understanding. To him belongs eternal praise." Also, see Proverbs 9:10.

Benefit # 3: The fear of the Lord brings prosperity to you and your children

When you fear the Lord, you prosper in everything you do and everything will go well with you. Deuteronomy 5:20, says, "O, that their hearts would be inclined to fear me and keep all my commands so that it might go well with them and their children forever.

Benefit # 4: The fear of the Lord is for your good

In Deuteronomy 10:12, we read, "And now O Israel, what does the Lord your God ask of you, but to fear the Lord your God, to walk in all his ways, to love him with all your heart, and with all your soul, and to observe the Lord's commands and decrees that I am giving you today for your own good."

Benefit # 5: The fear of the Lord gives you long life

If you desire to live a long life, then you must fear the Lord. Proverbs 10:27, reads, "The fear of the Lord adds length of life, but the years of the wicked are cut short."

Benefit # 6: You hate evil, pride, and arrogance when you fear the Lord

Proverbs 8:13, reads, "The fear of the Lord is to hate evil. I hate pride, and arrogance, evil behavior and perverse speech." It keeps you from speaking careless, cursing and dirty words.

Benefit # 7: Your sin is atoned for by the fear of the Lord

Proverbs 16:6, "Through love and faithfulness sin is atoned for, through the fear of the Lord, a man avoids evil."

Benefit # 8: The fear of the Lord protects you from troubles

Proverbs 19:23, "The fear of the Lord leads to life. Then one rests, content, untouched by troubles."

Benefit # 9: You prosper through the fear of the Lord. He instructs you and your descendants will inherit the land

Psalm 25:12 reads, "Who is the man that fears the Lord? He will instruct him in the ways chosen for him. He will spend his days in prosperity and his descendants will inherit the land."

Benefit # 10: The Lord confides in you and makes His covenant with you

Psalm 25:14, "The Lord confides in those who fear him, he makes his covenant known to them."

The Word of God has given you numerous counsels on how to confront fear and defeat it. When you pray, you must not allow negative fear to paralyze you any longer, because the Word of God has delivered you from all your fears. And all your fear means all your fear, no exceptions. All you need to do is to believe it without a doubt.

The Lord has also given you many benefits and promises when you fear Him, and believe that God is able to keep and fulfill His promises. You must trust Him by faith and have confidence in Him. You also must believe that God has given you victory over negative fear through His Word. Negative fear comes from the devil. Stay away from it. Positive fear comes from the Lord. Stay close to it because the promises and benefits, will transform your life. All of this will come to fruition if you pray and do not doubt. The doubt problem is the next topic of discussion.

Questions for Reflection

Instruction: React to the issue of fear.

1. What is fear?

_____
_____
_____

2. What are the differences between positive and negative fear?

_____
_____
_____

3. What did the Lord do with all your fears?

_____
_____
_____

4. What are the benefits of positive fear?

_____
_____
_____

5. What methods would you use to confront negative fear?

_____

_____

_____

6. Why do most people cling to their fears?

_____

_____

_____

Chapter Fourteen

Pray: The Faith Factor

**Now faith is being sure of what we hope for and
certain of what we do not see.
(Hebrews 11:1)**

The role faith plays in our prayer life cannot be underestimated. Prayer without faith produces zero results,
and prayer with faith produces maximum benefits and
rewards from God. The Bible makes it clears that there is a
definite connection between faith, the Word of God, and the
outcome of our prayer. But before highlighting the connec-
tions, we must focus on several fundamental truths about
faith in Hebrews chapter 11. Let us take a walk through the
School of Faith and meet some of the champions of faith,
whose encounters with God will challenge us and lead us to
discover profound treasures God has reserved for us when
we have faith in Him alone.

Fundamental truth # 1: Faith believes God

This truth is based on the premise that God exists and He created the universe by His spoken command. So, anyone who comes to Him must first believe that He exists. In other words, before you attempt to pray, you must first establish in your mind experientially that God exists and you believe Him and the power of His creative Word. (v.2&6)

Fundamental truth # 2: Faith pleases God

Evident in this truth is the fact that, "without faith, it is impossible to please God" (v.6a). For all practical purposes, if you do not have faith in God, then you cannot please Him, even when you try to get a prayer going, and any prayer that is not based on faith in God may be totally without value. But why is it impossible to please God without faith?

Fundamental truth # 3: Faith rewards

It is impossible to please God without faith because, "… anyone who comes to him (God), must believe that he exists and he rewards those who earnestly seek him." (v.6b)

If you expect a favorable reward from God when you pray, it is imperative to believe that He exists at all times, past, present and future, and He rewards positively and favorably at all times, past, present and future. In other words, He rewards us in His eternal present.

Fundamental truth # 4: Faith is commended

What could be more gratifying to us than when God commends us for our faith in Him? But our commendation is connected to our commitment to please Him. We can please God when we obey His commands by faith. For example, Abel was commended as a righteous man who offered a better sacrifice to God than Cain. "God spoke well of his offering."(v.4) Enoch was commended because he walked with God and pleased Him. (v.5) The other heroes of faith who did not even receive their promise were commended.

Fundamental truth # 5: Faith Produces salvation

Speaking about faith and righteousness, we take a walk with Noah. He was righteous, blameless among the people of his time, and he walked with God. He also found favor in the eyes of the Lord (Genesis 6:8). Noah feared the Lord. In holy fear, Noah obeyed the Lord and built the ark that saved him and his family from the flood that destroyed the people of Noah's time. Genesis 7:1 reads, The Lord then said to Noah, "Go into the ark, you and your whole family, because I have found you righteous in this generation." Noah was found righteous because he believed God by faith and acted by faith in response to God's command. By faith, Noah condemned the world and became heir of the righteousness that comes by faith (Hebrews 11:7). Noah's faith in God produced salvation. His faith brought him in right standing before God. In other words, God commended Noah because He found him righteous and through him saved his whole family. God could use one person who knows Christ to save a whole family. If God did it for Noah, He can do it for you. Ephesians 2:8 reads, "For by grace you have been saved through faith — and that not from yourselves, it is the gift of God — not by works, so that no one can boast."

Fundamental truth # 6: Faith is forward looking

Sometimes we get fixated on the now, and frequently we seem to forget that God is also the God of now and the future. But we need to understand that our now faith has its future companion and benefits. We have examples that ought to direct our focus to faith in a future mode. You see, "by faith Isaac blessed Jacob and Esau in regards to their future" (v.20). Similarly, "by faith Jacob, when he was dying, blessed each of Joseph's sons, and worshiped as he leaned on the top of his staff." (v.21) Also, "by faith Joseph, when his end was near, spoke about the exodus of the Israelites from Egypt and gave instructions about his bones" (v.22). They were to take his bones from Egypt to Israel.

Fundamental truth # 7: Faith demands obedience

Today, technology has made it easy for us to locate driving directions when we drive from one city to another or even from one state to another. We could use a road map, print out a travel direction from a computer for a MapQuest. Those who have vehicles that are equipped with a GPS compass can easily use it to locate their direction. These technologies are designed to help us arrive at our destination with minimum difficulty.

But could you imagine how Abraham may have felt when God called him to go to a place he had no idea where it was? Abraham did not have the luxury of today's technology and did not have anyone to ask for direction. But God was his GPS technology, his MapQuest, his compass and his direction provider.

Sometimes, we may not fully see or understand where God is taking us, but we ought to believe by faith that He is able to take us to the destination He has designed and purposed for us with all its challenges, advantages, benefits and rewards. However, it is important that we listen when He tells us to go, even if we do not have all the details or when all the instructions may not be fully humanly comprehended. But He will guide us all the way until we arrive at our destination. When we get there, then we will have a testimony. Are you ready to accept God's direction even when the direction is not clear?

That is what happened to Abraham. "By faith Abraham, when he was called to go to a place he would later receive as an inheritance, obeyed and went, even though he did not know where he was going.... For he was looking forward to a city with foundations, whose architect and builder is God." (v.8&10) What if God called you in the same manner He called Abraham, to do something you have no idea where it is headed or what the outcome would be, would you do it?

Abraham obeyed God and went without hesitation, without fully understanding all the implications, without knowing when he would receive the inheritance, without knowing when the promise would be fulfilled. Abraham lived like a stranger in a foreign land. He lived in temporary tents, as did Isaac and Jacob, who were heirs to the same promise. In spite of what appeared to be uncertain, Abraham obeyed God and eventually, the promise was fulfilled and he received the inheritance. Are you prepared to obey God once He has called you and told you what to do? Your inheritance is in your obedience, and your obedience confirms your faith in God.

Fundamental truth # 8: Faith challenges our patience

We don't like waiting. Sometimes it feels like God has forgotten us. We learned this lesson earlier with Hannah's experience with God. Hannah prayed and waited for many years before she had a son. Like Hannah, Abraham waited for many years before Isaac, the son of God's promise, was born. What happened?

When God sent Abraham out of Ur of the Chaldeans, he promised Abraham that he would possess the land of Canaan, he would have many descendants, and his offspring would become a great nation. The fulfillment of this promise would bring him great joy.

But after ten years, God still hadn't delivered on His promise (Genesis chapter 12). Take a look at what transpired.

- Abraham left his family and country
- God promised to bless him and his descendants
- Abraham lived through a time of famine
- He feared Pharaoh and lied to him
- He encountered family conflict and separated from Lot, his nephew
- He fought to rescue Lot when he was kidnapped
- He still had no son

After ten years, Abraham was not sure about the promise. Genesis 15:1, 5-6 reads, "After this, the Word of the Lord came to Abram in a vision, "Do not be afraid Abram, I am your shield, your very great reward." He took him outside and said, "Look up at the heaven and count the stars, if indeed you can count them." Then he said to him, "So shall your offspring be." Great promise, but remember, God is not in a hurry to do anything.

Fundamental truth # 9: Faith defeats doubt

Even after God's reassurance, Abraham still was not sure of what would happen.

The enemy planted a moment of doubt in Abraham's mind. And in response to the enemy's lie, Abraham and Sarah took matters into their own hands and had an illegitimate son through Sarah's maidservant. But God's ways and times are not like ours. Even though it may seem like a long time to us, God always does the right thing in His appointed time.

To complicate matters even more. Abraham and his wife, Sarah, wondered at the possibility of bearing a son in their old age. For them, the human timetable for bearing a child had passed a long time ago. But a human timetable is not compatible with God's timetable. Abraham was 99 years old and Sarah was 90 years old. Genesis 17:16-17 reads, God also said to Abraham, "As for Sarai your wife, you are no longer to call her Sarai, her name will be Sarah. I will bless her and will surely give you a son by her....Abraham fell facedown, he laughed and said to himself, 'Will a son be born to a man a hundred years old? Will Sarah bear a child at the age of ninety?'"

Abraham and Sarah did not understand that faith and doubt are mutually exclusive. We also have to understand this principle when we pray. We have to ensure that nothing interferes with our faith. And we need to avoid the kind of entrapment Abraham and Sarah had when they took matters into their own hands. When we pray, we need to affirm our prayer to God and ask Him for everything that is good. And God will always do what is right for us, even when what He says appears to be absurd or does not make sense to us.

But Abraham and Sarah experienced the paradox of hope in their encounter with God. They had faith against all hope. In human terms, time ran out, but in God's terms, time is timeless. Speaking about Abraham's faith in God, we could confirm that God has the power to create life where there is no life. Romans 4:17-18 reads, "He (Abraham) is our father in the sight of God, in whom he believed—God who gave life to the dead and calls things that are not as if they were. Against all hope, Abraham in hope believed and so became the father of nations, just as it had been said, to him so shall your offspring be." Similarly, when we encounter our own paradox of faith and hope, we must believe that God is able to hear our prayer and do what is right for us, even when and how He does it may not make sense to us. Do you believe it? Then trust Him to do what He said He will do.

Fundamental truth # 10: Faith is tested

When we think about one of the greatest tests of faith in the Bible, no one comes to mind but Abraham. He had gotten over his paradox of faith and hope against hope with having a son at 100 years old. And 13 years later, something tragic is about to happen to his only son. But that tragedy will not happen by an accident or by chance. He is to kill his only son. Amazing! Abraham in disbelief would not dare to share this predicament he is facing with his wife Sarah. Imagine what Sarah will be thinking if such bad news was broken to her. She might as well have lived out the rest of her old age without a son. But when God spoke, even when what He said might have sounded absurd, Abraham listened and obeyed. Wow! What happened?

God called Abraham and told him to sacrifice his only son. Genesis 22:2 reads, "Then God said, 'Take your son, your only son, Isaac whom you love, and go to the region of Moraiah. Sacrifice him there as a burnt offering on one of the mountains I will tell you about.'" This was serious business. God did not leave room for Abraham to misunderstand the command. God emphasized the instruction, "Take your son, your only son Isaac." God did not allow him room to think about someone else. There was only one voice that could not be mistaken and one direct instruction.

In obedience, Abraham, without question, prepared to undertake the ultimate act of faith that marked and credited him as the father of faith. Hebrews 11:17-19 reads, "By faith Abraham, when God tested him, offered Isaac as a sacrifice. He who had received the promise was about to sacrifice his one and only son, even though God had said to him, "It is through Isaac that your offspring will be reckoned." Abraham reasoned that God could raise the dead, and figuratively, he did receive Isaac back from death."

Because of Abraham's act of obedience, God instructed him not to lay a hand on Isaac, his only son, and instead, provided a ram as a substitute for Isaac. "An angel of the Lord called out to him from heaven, 'Abraham! Abraham! Do not lay a hand on the boy,' he said, 'do not do anything to him. Now I know that you fear God, because you have not withheld from me your son, your only son.'" (v.11) Abraham sacrificed the ram instead of Isaac and called the place of slaughter or sacrifice, "The Lord Will Provide." (v. 14) What an incredible test and an amazing act of faith and trust in God.

Just as God tested Abraham's faith, so He will test our faith in Him sometimes. But when that test comes, will you respond as Abraham did in obedience, even when what God is asking you to do may appear to be totally absurd? That is the challenging question. Think about it as you engage in your own prayer and faith walk alone with God.

Fundamental truth # 11: Faith gives up the safe zone

Sometimes we prefer to live most of our life holding on to our comfort and safe zones. But faith in God challenges us to live beyond our safe zone. The experience of Moses gives us a template on how to live beyond our safe zone. Moses was born into uncertainty, but after his mother put him in God's hands, Pharaoh's daughter raised him in the comfort of the king's palace. When he was forty, he left the safe zone and stepped out by faith on his own to do something great for his people. But when he killed an Egyptian in defense of a Hebrew, Pharaoh wanted to kill him and he fled, leaving his comfort zone.

After Moses left Egypt, he spent the next forty years in the Midian desert taking care of sheep. He liked the shepherd experience and became comfortable with the shepherd life-style, and the desert became another safe zone for him. But after a while, Jethro took him into his home and he became a partner in Jethro's business and eventually became his heir apparent, because Jethro had no son. Here Moses lived a comfortable life. All this time he was transiting from one experience to another, God had a different plan. Moses' life was about to change forever.

Moses' call and his excuses

When God called Moses from the burning bush in Exodus chapter 3, and told him to leave his comfort zone and go back to Egypt to accomplish God's eternal purpose, which was to lead the Israelites out of slavery and bondage, Moses felt totally unqualified, inadequate, and insecure to perform such a magnanimous task. So he had many questions. He had excuses. But God had all the right answers. Here are Moses' excuses and God's answers:

Excuse # 1: Not me

But Moses said to God, "Who am I, that I should go to Pharaoh and bring the Israelites out of Egypt?" (Exodus 3:11)

God answers: I will be with you

And God said, "I will be with you." (v.12)

Excuse # 2: I don't know what to say

Moses said to God, "Suppose I go to the Israelites and say to them, 'The God of your fathers has sent me to you,' and they ask me, 'What is his name?' then what shall I tell them?" (v.13)

God answers: I AM WHO I AM

God said to Moses, "I AM WHO I AM. This is what you are to say to the Israelites: 'I AM has sent me to you.'" (v. 14) God also said to Moses, "Say to the Israelites, 'The Lord, the God of your fathers, the God of Abraham, the God of Isaac, and the God of Jacob has sent me to you.' This is my name forever, the name by which I am to be remembered from generation to generation." (v. 15)

Excuse # 3: What if they don't believe me?

Moses answered, "What if they do not believe me or listen to me and say, 'The Lord did not appear to you?' What will I do?" (Exodus 4:1)

God answers: I will give you a sign

Then the Lord said to him, "What is that in your hand?" "A staff," he replied. The Lord said, "Throw it on the ground." (v.1-3). When Moses threw the staff on the ground it turned into a snake. Moses was afraid and ran away. But the Lord told him to pick the snake up and Moses picked it up and the snake turned into Moses' staff. The Lord performed other signs for Moses. (v. 6-9)

Excuse # 4: I can't speak

Moses said to the Lord, "O Lord, I have never been eloquent, neither in the past nor since you have spoken to your servant. I am slow to speak and tongue." (4:10)

God answers: I gave man mouth and tongue

The Lord said to Moses, "Who gave man his mouth? Who makes him deaf and mute? Who gave him sight, or makes him blind? Is it not I the Lord? Now go, I will help you speak and will teach you what to say." (4:11-12)

Excuse # 5: I can't do it, send someone else

Moses said to the Lord, "O Lord, please send someone else to do it." (4:13)

God answers: Well, what about Aaron

The Lord was angry with Moses and said, "What about your brother, Aaron the Levite? I know he can speak well. He is on his way to meet you. You shall speak to him and put Words in his mouth. I will help both of you speak, and will teach you what to do. He will speak to the people for you and it will be as if he were your mouth and as if you were God to him." After this last answer from God, Moses returned to Jethro's house in preparation for his journey back to Egypt to lead the Israelites from slavery out of Egypt. In doing that, he agreed to answer God's call to leave his comfort and safe zone.

In every way we are like Moses. How many times has God called us to a task or a mission and we drum up all sorts of excuses why it is not us that the Lord has called? Who among us have not said to God like Moses did, "O Lord, I can't do this or that, please send someone else"? Why?, because we are comfortable with where we are now. We are living in our safe zone. But we must realize that no amount of excuse will derail God's purpose and the destiny He has set for us. It may appear as if we are delaying God's vision. No! God is not in a hurry about anything. When His appointed time comes, He will accomplish His purpose in spite of our numerous excuses. Our comfort or safe zone is a dangerous place to be. We might as well leave it alone by faith.

Fundamental truth # 12: Faith does not compromise

Something unique and transforming happened to Moses when the Lord caused him to abandon his excuses and surrender to His call. A change he never thought was possible took place in dramatic ways in his life. Instead of depending on his ability to make intellectually reasonable excuses, he surrendered to God's call by faith. His life would never be the same again. Moses, the one who gave every excuse to avoid God's call, became an uncompromising champion leader of God's people. Hebrews 11:24-26 reads, "By faith Moses, when he had grown up, refused to be known as the son of Pharaoh's daughter. He chose to be mistreated along with the people of God rather than to enjoy the pleasures of sin for a short time. He regarded disgrace for the sake of Christ as of greater value than the treasures of Egypt, because he was looking ahead to his reward."

Faith in God was the engine that propelled Moses to discover his true identity. In other words, Moses found his real self and his true identity after he surrendered to God. Moses knew now that he was culturally a Jew. This fresh understanding of who he was convinced him to take some dramatic action. How?

Dramatic action # 1: He would not compromise his heritage

Moses refused to be known any longer as the son of Pharaoh's daughter.

Dramatic action # 2: He would not compromise with sin

Moses consciously chose to suffer with the people of God, no matter how long it took, instead of enjoying the pleasure of sin in Egypt for even a short time.

Dramatic action # 3: He would not compromise his reward

Moses regarded disgrace for the sake of Christ of greater value than the treasures of Egypt, because he was looking forward to God's best reward.

Moses could not have been able to take these dramatic actions that changed his life if he had not surrendered his life in obedience to God's call. In his pre-call state, he had all the excuses, but in his faith state, he found his true identify in God and demonstrated that no matter how good it may have been in Egypt, when he trusted God by faith he knew that he got the best in God. And he had no room for compromise. Even so for us, when we answer God's call in Christ Jesus and He gives us an assignment, we should be prepared to make dramatic decisions and changes that look forward to God's best reward for us. Remember, no compromises.

Fundamental truth # 13: Faith conquers battles

There is nothing imaginable in life's battles that faith in God cannot conquer. Faith in God conquers physical, emotional, psychological and spiritual battles. The Bible has numerous examples of people who conquered kingdoms, administered justice, shut the mouths of lions, quenched the fury of flames, escaped the edge of the sword, whose weakness was turned into strength and who became powerful in battle and routed foreign armies. Here is a short list of the people in Hebrews 11:32-33, "And what more shall I say, I do not have time to tell about Gideon, Samson, Jephthah, David, Samuel and the prophets..." These warriors and many others, like Joshua, won their battles by faith in God. Their victories were not won because of their massive armies or sophisticated superior weaponry, but by faith.

While these warriors won military combats by faith, those who were physically weak became strong because the Lord turned their weakness into strength and they became powerful. They put their enemies in disarray. In the same way, if we confront our battles by faith in God, we will have the victories, and even when we are weak, the Lord will turn our weakness into strength.

Fundamental truth # 14: Faith endures suffering

Suffering generates very perplexing and puzzling questions in people's minds about the love and power of God to relieve suffering. Whether the suffering is physical, mental, psychological or emotional, people have always wondered at the enormous pain we experience when we suffer from tragedy, sickness, persecution, ridicule, distress, humiliation, depression, hatred, rejection, hurt, death of a loved one, or other forms of suffering that befalls us.

While some people are bewildered at the magnitude of some suffering, some scholars and theologians believe that suffering is a mystery that we cannot fully understand. Others believe that suffering, in whatever form it takes, is permitted by God, and we just have to learn how to cope with it. But some have asked, if God is love and all powerful, why does He allow us to suffer? Why can't He end suffering?

As legitimate and challenging as these questions may be, the reality is that there are no easy human answers. We may ask where is God when we are hurting? Where is God when we are suffering? Someone figured out an answer that defies all human understanding, that God was in the same place He was when His Son Jesus Christ was suffering pain on the cross. But God was also suffering pain with His Son. In the same way, God does not abandon us when we suffer. He suffers with us and comforts us in our suffering. The Apostle Paul testifies to the reason God comforts us. II Corinthians 1:3-6, reads, "Praise be to the God and Father of our Lord Jesus Christ, the Father of compassion and the God of all comfort, who comforts us in all our troubles, so that we can comfort those in any trouble, with the comfort we ourselves have received from God. For just as the suffering of Christ flows over into our lives, so also through Christ our comfort overflows. If we are distressed, it is for your comfort and salvation. If we are comforted, it is for your comfort, which produces in you patient endurance of the same suffering we suffer." In other words, our suffering is not in vain. God prepares us to become faith partners with those who suffer the same things we had suffered, from which God had given us comfort and victory.

Yes, God is love and all-powerful. He has power to end all pain. However, when and how He ends our pain is totally dependent on Him. Sometimes, we may not be pleased with how our suffering ends, but in spite of how it ends, our suffering is used to test our faith in God. The test is for our own good, to teach us how to persevere, mature, and when our test is complete, in Christ, God commends us even when we have not received what had been promised us now. James 1:24 reads, "Consider it joy, my brothers, whenever you face trials of many kinds, because you know that the testing of your faith develops perseverance. Perseverance must finish its work, so that you may be mature and complete and lacking nothing." But sometimes we don't really think much about perseverance. We don't care much about waiting on God. We don't like to stay in His faith training school. We want everything now, but do you know that some of the great champions of faith we have been discussing in Hebrews 11 were commended by God, even though they never received what they were promised while they lived? Shocking!

You see, what has all this got to do with faith and prayer? Frequently, we get upset with God when we have prayed and asked God for something. It does not really matter what it is we have asked Him to give or do for us, but are we willing to accept His commendation even when we have not received what He promised?

Take a look at what happened to some of those who trusted God by faith, but never received their promise. Hebrews 11:36-40 reads, "Some faced jeers and flogging, while still others were chained, and put in prison. They were stoned, they were sawed into two, they were put to death by the sword. They went about in sheepskins, and goatskins, destitute, persecuted, and mistreated—the world was not worthy of them. They wandered in deserts and mountains, and in caves and holes in the ground. These were all commended for their faith, yet none of them received what was promised. God had planned something better for us, so that only together with us will they be made perfect."

It is amazing to know that all the heroes of faith, including those who received what they were promised and those who did not receive their promise, were commended because of their faith in God. What a wonderful testimony. Can you please, praise, and worship God in your exercise of faith, even when you have not received what was promised? Do you expect God to commend you? This is the faith factor. But what is faith?

What is Faith?

Hebrews 11:1 gives us the answer, "Now faith is being sure of what we hope for and certain of what we do not see." The operative words in this definition are "sure," "hope," and "certain." The word that is not part of faith is "doubt." All three operative words are positive. Doubt is eliminated. Doubt has a negative connotation. In other words, faith and doubt are mutually exclusive. Faith is positive and doubt is negative. You cannot be sure and certain about something, and doubt at the same time. Being sure and certain about anything should confirm the absence of doubt. When you are sure and certain about something, even a dispute cannot change what is sure and certain.

When we activate our faith, it starts operating now and culminates in the future. So now faith is actualized in the future. In other words, faith is forward looking, as we had seen earlier. As we actualize our faith, we reinforce and confirm our confidence in God that He will commend us and reward us with His promises. Hebrews 10:35-36 reads, "So do not throw away your confidence, it will be richly rewarded. You need to persevere so that when you have done the will of God, (which is to please Him) you will receive what he has promised."

The other operative component of faith is "**hope.**"

What is hope?

Hope is the future companion of faith. It is looking forward in expectation for something, a promise, even though you have not seen or received it. And for this reason, every prayer we say is an expression of hope. If you do not have hope, then there is nothing to look forward to. Henri Nouwen puts is this way, "A man (person) who expects nothing from the future cannot pray" He says in the words of Bertold Brecht, "As it is it will stay, what we want will never come." For the person who expects nothing, life stands still. The person is spiritually dead. But hope looks ahead toward that which is not yet. To go fearlessly into things without knowing how they will turn out, and to keep on going even when something does not work the first time, the second time, even the third time, and to have faith that God will ultimately work it out for your good—now that is hope. Because hope is based on the premise that God gives only what is good. And so your prayer should be directed not to the gift, but to God who is the giver of all good gifts. And whenever we pray with hope, we put our lives in God's hands. When what we expected is actualized by faith, now we move on to the next faith project. Hope prompts you to wait patiently for what has been promised. Romans 6:24 reads, "But hope that is seen is not hope at all. Who hopes for what he already has? But if we hope for what we do not yet have, we wait for it patently."

So whatever you have asked from God, you have to wait for it patiently, for in due time, it will be manifested. If you have faith in God, then you should not doubt anything God has said in His Word. When you are sure about anything, there should be no reason to doubt. You cannot have faith and doubt simultaneously. It should be either faith or doubt. But your choice every time should be faith. Why?

Faith and Doubt Are Mutually Exclusive

How faith impacts our prayer life can be dramatic in many ways. And since faith and doubt are mutually exclusive, you have to be sure that nothing interferes with your faith. First, when you pray, you must be sure to affirm your prayer to God and ask Him for everything that is good. You must also make sure that your affirmation guarantees the absence of doubt. And if you lack wisdom when you pray, you must ask God to give it to you to help you articulate your prayer in God's terms. James 1:5-8 reads, "If anyone of you lacks wisdom, he should ask God who gives generously to all without finding fault and it will be given to him. But when he asks, he must believe and not doubt, because he who doubts is like a wave of the sea, blown and tossed by the wind. That man should not think he will receive anything from the Lord, he is a double-minded man, unstable in all he does."

Second, when you pray, the word you speak must validate your faith and your faith must be confirmed by the Word of God. Our Lord Jesus stressed this vital relationship between your faith and the Word of God in His teaching on the withered fig tree. And this account illustrates the power inherent in the spoken word. This is how it happened.

How a Fig Tree Died

Our Lord Jesus taught the profound truth about faith, when He made the connection between the spoken Word and faith. In Matthew 21:18-20, "Early in the morning, Jesus was on his way back to the city, and he was hungry. Seeing a fig tree by the road, he went up to it but found nothing on it except leaves. Then he said to it, 'May you never bear fruit again.' Immediately, the tree withered. When his disciples saw this, they were amazed. 'How did the fig tree wither so quickly?' they asked. Jesus replied, 'I tell you the truth, if you have faith and do not doubt, not only can you do what was done to the fig tree, but also you can say to this mountain, "You throw yourself into the sea," and it will be done. If you believe, you will receive what you ask for in prayer.'"

In this account, Jesus made the connection between belief, faith, and the Word. None of these three elements could act alone or in isolation. All three elements had to be present to achieve and produce the expected outcome. In other words, for you to realize the full outcome or impact of your faith, you must speak the Word, believe in the Word, and believe that what you have spoken will happen and that you will receive what you asked for in prayer. But why is what is spoken so important?

Life and Death belong to the Tongue

The dead fig tree account confirms and validates a biblical principle that states that what the tongue speaks could result into life or death. Proverbs 18:21 says, "The tongue has the power of life and death, and those who love it will eat the fruit." This was manifested with the withered fig tree account. Jesus spoke death and the tree died. Similarly, you can speak life or death, and it will happen. So we need to be cautious about what we say. But what we say may have other outcomes.

The Tongue can put Things in Motion

Jesus also taught about **the principle of kinesics or motion.** This principle confirms the fact that what we speak has the power to set things in motion. In other words, you have the power to speak life even to inanimate objects, and they will become alive, move and settle themselves where you have commanded them to go or be. Conversely, you can speak to a dead thing and it will come to life. However, what you speak will happen only if you believe it and have faith and not doubt. Romans 4:17-18, speaking about Abraham's faith, God confirms God's power to create life where there is no life. "He (Abraham) is our Father in the sight of God in whom he believed—God who gave life to the dead and calls things that are not as though they were. Against all hope, Abraham in hope believed and so became the father of nations, just as it had been said to him. So shall your offspring be." What an amazing act of faith.

How Big Should Faith in Motion be?

Some have asked, how big should our faith in motion be? How big should the faith that is capable of setting things in motion be? How big should the faith that speaks life and death be? Jesus answered these questions with the story about the healing of a young boy who had seizures, in Matthew 17:14-21, "When they came to the crowd, a man approached Jesus and knelt before him, 'Lord, have mercy on my son,' he said. 'He has seizures, and suffering greatly. He often falls into the fire and into the water. I brought him to your disciples, but they could not heal him.'

Jesus respond, "O unbelieving and perverse generation, how long shall I put up with you? Bring the boy here to me." Jesus rebuked the demon and it came out of the boy and he was healed from that moment." Then the disciples came to Jesus in private and asked, "Why couldn't we drive it out?" He replied, "Because you have so little faith, I tell you the truth, if you have faith as small as a mustard seed, you can say to the mountain, 'Move from here to there, and it will move.' Nothing will be impossible for you."

In this encounter, Jesus would not tolerate unbelief from His disciples. Similarly, He would not put up with the negative attitudes of any unbelieving generation. Jesus expressed frustration at the lack of faith exhibited by His disciples after he had taught them by action, in stories and parables, in private and in public, and they still would not take responsibility. Jesus expected faith in action from them, but they were a complete disappointment to Him. You see, unbelief and inaction contradicts everything Jesus taught them. His disciples failed woefully at an opportunity they had to demonstrate faith in action. No wonder today there are many who would not act in faith.

Quality Faith, not Quantity Faith

While Jesus emphasized quality faith, His disciples were thinking about quantity faith. They thought that they had to have a huge monstrous faith to rebuke and cast out a demon. But what they needed was quality faith. Quality faith does not doubt the Word of God or the power of the spoken Word of God. If they had quality faith even as small as the smallest of all seeds, they would have been able to rebuke the demon and it would have left the young boy. They failed to understand that quality faith is not determined by size or how big it is, but by believing and trusting the Lord, who gives only quality faith.

But how does quality faith work?

Work Your Mustard Seed Faith

How mustard seed faith works is that you have to work it. Jesus challenged His disciples because of their unbelief, inaction, and lack of quality faith. He compared quality faith to a mustard seed faith, which His disciples didn't even have. Mustard seed faith is quality, potent, vibrant and active faith. Mustard seed faith speaks to life and generates life. Mustard seed faith supersedes all conventional wisdom and demolishes all the status quo. It moves us from our comfort and safe zone to a new zone of action. It challenges us to try things we have not done before. Mustard seed faith disarms you from depending on yourself, and propels you to direct your trust in God.

Mustard seed faith is anchored in conviction and confidence in God. It is capable of driving out demons, breaking yokes and shackles. It removes all demonic restrictions, limitations, obstacles, and what hinders us, and subjects them under the authority of the Word of God and the name of Jesus. This is the kind of faith you need to exercise without reservations or doubt. Now act on your mustard seed faith and let it work for you as you work it by faith. Speak life to your circumstances and watch it come to be. You do not need to have more faith, you only need to work your mustard seed faith and see it blossom and grow into faith in action. Put mustard seed faith into action in your prayers. How?

Faith Prayer in Action

Faith that works must be validated by action. The Bible made it clear that faith without works is dead. James 2:14 reads, "What good is it, my brothers, if a man claims he has faith but has no deeds. Can his faith save him? ...In the same way, faith by itself, if not accompanied with action, is dead." (see James 2:7). In other words, faith cannot stand alone. We cannot isolate it from works. Faith must be complemented by good deeds, acts of kindness, helping the poor, the widow, the orphan, the destitute, the disadvantaged, the sick, the homeless, those in captivity, and in prison, etc. But what has this got to do with prayer? It has everything to do with prayer, because prayer demands action. You pray and act. You pray and do. If you prayed and never took any action, then your prayer may not produce any measurable outcome. You may ask, "How do you know that prayer without action is dead?" The answer is next.

Give Me a Break

Jack Canfield told a story of a man who goes to church and prays, "God I need a break. I need to win the state lottery. I'm counting on you, God." Having not won, the man returns to church a week later and once again prays, "God, about that state lottery, I've been kind to my wife, I have given up drinking. I've been really good. Give me a break. Let me win the lottery."

A week later, still no richer, he returns to pray once again, "God, I don't seem to be getting through to you on the state lottery thing. I've been using positive self-talk, saying affirmations and visualizing the money. Give me a break, God, let me win the lottery." Suddenly, the heavens open up, white light and heavenly music flood into the church, and a deep voice says, "My son, give me a break. Buy a lottery ticket."

This prayer illustrates an erroneous attitude and a misunderstanding some people have about how to pray and release the brakes in your life. The problem with the prayer is that first, the man trivialized the concept of prayer by focusing on a wish for immediate fulfillment instead of on faith. This kind of prayer has a Santa Claus mentality. In other words, the point of the prayer is on winning the lottery now, and when this fails, disappointment sets in. Second, there is no indication or evidence that the man had confidence or trust in his prayer. The very language he used in the prayer is a clear demonstration of going through the motions. The man focused all his attention on the gift, and not on God who gives the gift. Third, this prayer was wrapped up in self-righteousness. The man claims to have done everything right, and therefore deserves favor from God. But one thing was obvious: the man never took action. He never bought a ticket. He failed to realize that nothing happens until you take action.

The faith and hope factor summons us to understand that when we pray, we are surrendering our desires, dreams, our hopes to God, and asking Him to act in His faithfulness. When we pray, we are releasing our suffering, pain, hurt, distress, disappointments, trials, tragedies, sickness, successes and failures to Him. He sets us free to put our lives in His Hands by faith.

Questions for Reflection

Instruction: Respond to faith issues.

1. What is faith?

_____
_____
_____
_____

2. What are the fundamental truths about faith?

_____
_____
_____
_____

3. How did the heroes of faith in the school of faith impact your prayer?

_____
_____
_____
_____

4. Why is faith and doubt mutually exclusive?

_____

_____

_____

_____

5. What is the mustard seed faith and how do you work it?

_____

_____

_____

_____

6. Why is the power of life and death in the tongue?

_____

_____

_____

_____

7. What is hope?

_____

_____

_____

_____

8. What do faith, hope and confidence have in common?

_____

_____

_____

_____

Chapter Fifteen

Pray: Release The Brakes Factor

Do not be anxious about anything, but in everything, by prayer and petition, with thanksgiving, present your requests to God. And the peace of God, which transcends all understanding, will guard your hearts and your minds in Christ Jesus.
(Philippians 4:6-7)

Taking action after you have prayed requires you to release the brakes in your life. If you pray and ask God to give you a break, then you ought to be prepared to release the brakes that are restraining you from moving forward and taking action. And the brakes you ought to release may be negative fear, hatred, detachment, envy, pride, jealousy, greed, self-doubt, coveting, arrogance, procrastination, laziness, negativism, overly critical, nagging, blaming others for everything that has gone wrong but not yourself, staying in your comfort zone too long, harboring guilt, un-forgiveness, un-confessed sin, gossip, slander, resistance to change, clinging tight to the past hurt, etc. These kinds of brakes are toxic, choking and inhibitory. They are success killers. They result in all kinds of can't. You cannot genuinely pray to God and still hold unto your brakes.

You need to release these negative brakes and set yourself free from stagnation, and incapacitation. Negative thoughts cannot be reinforced. They have to be revamped by living in the faith zone and not in the safe zone, where there is inaction.

Releasing these prayer brakes in your life are not as easy as we may think, but it is possible when you allow God to enter into the center of your life and take control of your life. It becomes easier when you allow God to speak in your life, allow Him to touch the sensitive core of your being, allow Him to see that which you would rather leave in darkness, allow Him to open the center of your emotions.

You see, you will be able to make room for God when you allow Him to say something, to touch something, as you let Him into the place where your life has anchored in defense. Taking our natural defensive positions can restrict us from opening our lives to the Lord, to enter and make all the necessary changes for life and godliness.

The Clenched Fist

Henri Nouwen told a story about an old woman who was brought to a psychiatric center. She was wild, swinging at everything in sight, and scaring everyone, so much that the doctor took everything away from her. But she had one small coin, which she gripped in her clenched fist and would not give up. It took two men to pry open the squeezed hand. It was as though she would lose herself along with the coin. If they deprived her of that last possession, she would have nothing more and be nothing more. That was her fear.

This story illustrates how sometimes, we clench so tight to our hurts and fears because we are afraid to open our hearts, to let God in to release us from the bondage of un-confessed sin, guilt, un-forgiveness, and hatred. We are reluctant to give up our last coin of anger, pride, self-pity, stinginess, and even the sin that entangles us – selfish love, lust, fornication, idolatry, adultery, deceit, lying, cheating, manipulation, control, etc.

Sometimes we feel like we have forgotten our hurts and fear until the moment we are about to pray, then everything returns, the bitterness, the hate, the jealousy, the disappoint-ment, and the desire to get revenge. We hold these feeling in our hearts as if they were treasures we are reluctant to part with. How awful.

The problem with this is that we are making every effort to stay detached from what will release us from our prayer brakes and transform our lives. But the more we stay attached to what is repulsive, the more difficult it is for us to make room for God to heal our hurts and fears. This is not God's will for us. We must take the following actions to release the brakes in our lives.

The Process of Releasing Your Prayer Brakes

Action Point # 1: Do not be afraid to submit your fears to God

You should not be afraid of God, who wants to enter the place where you live. Don't be afraid to let God see what you are clinging to so anxiously. And you should not be afraid to offer your hate, bitterness, and disappointment to Him who reveals His love to you. Even if you know that you have very little to show, do not be afraid to let Him see it.

The Bible has numerous examples where God had encouraged leaders, prophets, kings and many people who served Him with this phrase, "Do not be afraid." When the Lord says to you, "Do not be afraid," you should believe His promise. For example, when the angel Gabriel went to Mary and announced, in Luke 1:28-30, "Greetings, you who are highly favored! The Lord is with you," Mary was greatly troubled at his words and wondered what kind of greeting this might be, but the angel said to her, "Do not be afraid Mary, you have found favor with God." Also, when an angel appeared to the shepherds and announced the birth of Christ in Luke 2:8-10, they were terrified. But the angel said to them, "Do not be afraid, I bring you good news of great joy that will be for all the people." In the two instances, both Mary and the shepherds expressed awe, inadequacy, vulnerability and fear of the Lord. But the Lord calmed their fears with His encouragement. Furthermore, the Psalmist was confident that the Lord was able to deliver him from all his fears. Psalm 34:4: "I sought the Lord and he answered me and he delivered me from all my fears."

There is another profound testimony from the Psalmist confirming his trust and confidence in God to alleviate his fear. Psalm 56:3-4: "When I am afraid, I will trust in you. In God whose Word I praise, in God I trust, I will not be afraid, what can mortal man do to me?" You also can be like the Psalmist, when you submit your fears and hurts to God in prayer and trust Him to heal you and encourage you with His promise, "Do not be afraid."

Action Point # 2: Be specific in what you ask

To activate your faith in prayer requires you to be specific in what you are asking God to do. But specificity is not by itself enough. Even the man who prayed to win a lottery was specific in what he asked, but he never bought a lottery ticket. He never took action.

Praying with specificity is an asset that enhances your prayer and keeps you focused on what you are asking from God. Also, being specific allows you to express your needs with clarity and precision. How?

Action Point # 3: Identify your need by name

Whatever the need may be — healing, financial, deliverance, freedom from addictive behavior, emotional, relational, social, economic, psychological, mental, etc. In other words, do not clutter your prayer requests with too many unspecified items. You cannot be vague. For example, all the people Jesus healed in the gospels came to Him with their specific needs.

Whether the people came by themselves or were brought to Him by others, one thing was clear: they named their specific problem and the Lord responded to the specific need, one at a time. It did not matter what kind of disease, sickness, condition or circumstance, the requests were specific.

Action Point # 4: Present your need to the Lord with confidence

When you go to pray, present your need to the Lord with confidence that He is able to do what you have asked. I John 5:14-15 says, "This is the confidence we have in approaching God, that if we ask anything according to his will, he hears us. And if we know that he hears us in whatever we ask, we know that we have what we asked of him"

Action Point # 5: Believe by faith that you have what you have asked

The requirements here are first, before we approach God, we must already have the conviction, faith, trust and confidence to ask according to His will as revealed in His Word, by the Holy Spirit. Second, we must know experientially not intellectually that He hears us always, not intermittently or occasionally. Third, we must know experientially by faith that we already have what we have asked for. We cannot present a problem to the Lord with doubt. Even if it has not manifested now, we still have the confidence that He is able to do what we have asked. Remember, faith and doubt are mutually exclusive. Only faith will make it happen.

Action Point # 6: Be obedient to do whatever the Lord asks you to do

The Bible says in I Samuel 15:22, "But Samuel replied, 'Does the Lord delight in burnt offerings and sacrifices, as much as obeying the voice of the Lord? To obey is better than sacrifice, and to heed is better than the fat of rams.'"

When you pray, you must be prepared to obey and do what the Lord has instructed you to do. The instructions may be to act in faith and obedience. For example, the people Jesus healed in the gospels trusted in Him by faith and acted on what He told them to do.

In other words, obedience activates action, and action validates obedience and faith. Both obedience and action are the bonds that complete and seal your faith in God. Consequently, you are able to receive all you have asked from God. In addition, you may pray as much as you want, but if you do not obey and act on what the Lord commanded, you may not receive what you have asked.

Action Point # 7: Be grateful to God for His rewards

There is something unique and special about gratitude, thankfulness and praise to God when He answers your prayer. It does not matter if God answered immediately, delayed, or said outright "not now," He has answered and we must thank Him in spite of how He answered. And we are assured that He will give us the best of what we have asked, because He gives only the best gifts. So praise Him at all times without exception. Psalm 34:1 reads, "I will extol the Lord at all times, his praise will always be on my lips." (No exceptions, no conditions, and no regrets.)

Praise the Lord, worship and glorify Him. And remember, you cannot worship Him and worry at the same time. Worship and worry are mutually exclusive. In other words, it is either worship or worry. While worship is an aroma to

God, worry is the stink of the devil. Stay away from worry. The Bible says in Matthew 6::27a, 31a, and 33, "Which of you by worrying can add a single hour to his life….So do not worry saying, 'What shall we eat?' or 'What shall we drink?' or 'What shall we wear?' …your heavenly Father knows that you need these things… But seek first the kingdom of God and his righteousness and all these things will be given to you as well."

Action Point # 8: Enter into His presence alone

In God's presence with Him alone is the place where you lay down your fears, hurts, disappointments, frustrations, sighs, humiliations, rejections, pains, hatred, insecurities, greed, envy, jealousy, deception, gossip, criticism, nagging, self-pity, meanness, control, un-forgiveness etc. How?

You prepare your mind to worship Him in prayer. The Bible counsels us to be still in His presence. Psalm 40:10 says, "Be still and know that I am God. I will be exalted among the nations. I will be exalted in the earth." You must also remember that you have entered His gates and courts, ready to worship Him with praise and adoration. Psalm 104:4 says, "Enter his gates with thanksgiving and his courts with praise, give thanks to him and praise his name."

Action Point # 9: Confess all known sin against God and people

Confession sets you free from guilt. You cannot harbor guilt and pray. Hebrews 10:22 reads, "Let us draw near to God with a sincere heart in full assurance of faith, having our hearts sprinkled (by the blood of Jesus) to cleanse us from a guilty conscience and having our bodies washed with pure water." Furthermore, you must appear before God with a pure heart. Psalm 32:5 says, "Then I acknowledged my sin to you and did not cover up my iniquity; I said, I will confess my transgressions to the Lord and you forgave me the guilt of my sin." Also Psalm 66:18 reads, "If I had cherished sin in my heart, the Lord would not have listened."

Action Point # 10: Forgive yourself and those who have sinned against you

An unforgiving spirit hinders prayer. So you have to forgive yourself, and no matter how deep the hurt and how serious the offense may have been, you must forgive. Realize that one of the hardest challenges you encounter is the determination to forgive those who hurt you. Someone you love or care about may have hurt you deep to the core of your being, bruised your sense of dignity and self-esteem, but you must still forgive. No matter how difficult it may be, your first step to healing lies in your ability to forgive. When you forgive yourself and the other, you release yourself from someone else holding you hostage and in bondage. And do not let the hurt linger, because the longer it lingers, the more your life is shattered, and the more it remains in shambles.

Action Point # 11: Ask God to help you release the brakes and heal you

What is left here is the victory you will claim in the Lord. Ask God to give you the power, fortitude, and grace to forgive and release all the negative brakes in order to transform your prayer life. When you let go, you have released yourself from someone else's control. Releasing the negative brakes becomes easier when you allow God to enter into the center of your life and take control, when you allow Him to speak in your life, when you allow Him to touch the sensitive core of your being, when you allow Him to see you just as you are, and to heal you.

And remember do not take vengeance for yourself. The Bible said in Romans 12:17-19, "Do not repay anyone evil for evil. Be careful to do what is right in the eyes of everybody. Do not take vengeance, my friends, but leave room for God's wrath, for it is written, 'It is mine to revenge, I will repay,' says the Lord." You see, when you have made room for God, you have allowed Him to say something special and touch something special, do something special in you.

Indeed, you would have released your prayer brakes and God would have transformed your life.

Questions for Reflection

Instruction: React with insight on releasing the brakes factor.

1. Why should we pray with open hands?

_____

_____

_____

2. What happens to our prayer when we cling to our comfort zones?

_____

_____

_____

3. What are the action points for releasing your prayer brakes?

_____

_____

_____

4. Why should we obey what God has asked us to do?

_____

_____

_____

5. What are those things we need to release to the Lord?

_____

_____

_____

6. What happens when we let the status quo go?

_____

_____

_____

_____

Chapter Sixteen

Pray: Action Strategies

**Be joyful always, pray continually, give thanks in
all circumstances for this is God's will for you in
Christ Jesus.**
(I Thessalonians 5:17-18)

Since you have taken the responsibility to read this
book, it is imperative that you endeavor to implement
the strategies and action tips to actualize your transforming
experience. Your attitude to prayer that transforms should be
characterized by humility, not pride or arrogance; faith, not
doubt; victory, not defeat; confidence, not distrust; love, not
hate; joy, not sadness; action, not inaction; power, not weakness; strength, not weariness; hope, not despair; praise, not
gloom; forgiveness, not un-forgiveness; worship, not worry;
truth, not falsehood; obedience, not disobedience; patience,
not hurry; focused, not confusion; success, not failure;

excellence, not mediocre; 'can do.' not 'can't do'; release the brakes, not holding onto your brakes; and much more. Know that all these can be accomplished through prayer. To maximize your benefits from God, you should implement these action tip steps.

Action tip # 1: Resist the devil

To claim the victory of a transformed prayer life, we need to resist the devil. In other words, we should not give the devil any loophole to discourage, hinder or disrupt us from having a victorious prayer life. The devil has a crafty way of cluttering our life and wearing us down with all kinds of irrelevant or trivial activities, such as too much sleep that cuts into our prayer time, going to bed late, watching TV, surfing the Internet, spending too much time on PLAYSTATION, reading all other kinds of romance literature, beauty magazines, homemakers books, men and women sports magazines, you name it, except reading the Word of God. I Peter 5:8-9 reads, "Be self-controlled and alert. Your enemy, the devil prowls around like a roaring lion, looking for someone to devour. Resist him, standing in the faith, because you know that your brothers throughout the world are undergoing the same kind of suffering." James 4:7 also reads, "Submit yourselves then to God. Resist the devil, and he will flee from you."

Resisting the devil requires us to make the full use of the power of the Word of God, which is our offensive and defensive weapon against the evil. We cannot resist him effectively if we do not read, study, and memorize the Word, so that when he attacks us, we are already equipped with the Word to launch a counter attack and defeat him.

Action tip # 2: Set up a daily convenient prayer time.

One attitude that stifles prayer is lack of planning. Effective prayer cannot be engaged in randomly. When you set prayer time, make sure you stick with it. However, do not be afraid to make changes when necessary. A praying person is like an athlete; you train, you persevere, you are focused, you endure, and the end results are worth it.

Action tip # 3: Select a portion of scripture, read, and meditate on it before you pray

This action is particularly important, because you need to listen to the Lord through His Word before you start speaking or waiting quietly before Him. It is imperative that you memorize the Word so you can recall it when you need it. Joshua 1:8 reads, "Do not let this Book of the law depart from your mouth. Meditate on it day and night, so that you may be careful to do everything written in it. Then you will be prosperous and successful." You see, this command comes with a promise, namely, prosperity and success. You cannot beat it.

Action tip # 4: Pray and listen to the Holy Spirit

Sometimes we rush to pray in the flesh. We go through the motions just to say we have prayed. This attitude is self-defeating, and there is no benefit to it. The Lord sent the Holy Spirit who dwells in us to help us to pray, because we sometimes do not know how to pray or what to say. This situation demands that we rely on the Holy Spirit to pray for us. Galatians 4:6 reads, "Because you are sons, God sent the Spirit of his Son into our hearts, the Spirit which calls out, 'Abba Father.' The same Spirit of God helps us in our weakness or our weak moments, when we do not know what to pray." Romans 8:26-27 also reads, "In the same way, the Spirit helps us in our weakness. We do not know what we ought to pray for, but the Spirit himself intercedes for us with groans that words cannot express. And he who searches our hearts knows the mind of the Spirit, because the Spirit intercedes for the saints in accordance with God's will."

Action tip # 5: Do not rush your prayer

Prayer is a special fellowship time alone with God. We should treat it with maximum reverence. We are in His presence to praise and worship Him. This is the time we have to express our love, concerns, fears, hurts, cries, distresses, pain, victories, successes, joys, weaknesses. We open up our total being to Him and He feels us with His love. In this situation, there is no need to hurry. We pray and wait for Him to act. You see, God is not in a hurry to do anything. The Psalmist attests to this in Psalm 40:1, "I waited patiently for the Lord; he turned to me and heard my cry." Pay attention to what the Psalmist said. These are words of wisdom.

Action tip # 6: Ask again and again

The unique thing about asking is that you have nothing to lose. The worst that can happen it that the person you are asking from may just say no. And that's all right. Move on to the next person. Even sometimes it does not hurt to ask the person you had asked before, who turned you down. He might change his mind. But God is not like that. He does not change His mind. He is the giver of all good gifts. The only thing we need to do is to set our focus on God the giver and not on the gift, because He gives us the best gifts. We open our hands and He fills them with wonderful gifts. But we should not be afraid to ask God repeatedly for His favor, mercy, and provisions. God is faithful and will do what He promised. Act on the principles of asking in this book, and wait for results.

Action tip # 7: Be humble

Prayer is about God, not about you or how well you can articulate words. It is not about impressing people in public prayer with your special tonal inflections. No, you are not impressing God, either. Prayer is not about seeking validation from people, because people's compliments last only for a moment and can quickly fizzle out into disdain, but when God validates you, it lasts forever. So humble yourselves when you pray, for God brings down the proud and exalts the humble. Matthew 23:12 confirms this. "For whoever exalts himself, will be humbled and whoever humbles himself will be exalted."

Action tip # 8: Do not give up

Quitting is not an option for anyone whose faith is anchored in the Lord. It does not matter how long it may take to receive what God has promise, do not quit, because there is no failure with God. A quitting spirit or attitude is the devil's weapon, used to discourage us from persevering to the end. The devil is a destroyer, and must not be allowed to invade and attack your prayer life. Even when the time of waiting is prolonged, you should never quit.

Action tip # 9: Activate your faith

We embarked on this prayer journey with the determination and conviction that only by faith in God can our prayer life be transformed. The Bible says, "We live by faith, not by sight." (II Corinthians 5:7) And when we activate our faith, it becomes the foundation for total surrender of our life to God. It becomes the only condition for receiving what God has promised. And without faith, it is impossible to please God, because anyone who comes to Him must believe that He exists and that He rewards those who earnestly seek Him. (Hebrews 11:6)

Finally, as we have come to the end of this journey on prayer, I must not fail to remind you that this book is written to transform your prayer life dramatically, so you can fully experience the power of God when you spend that special time alone in His presence. Above all, that you would have learned that the ultimate outcome of praying is to know that whatever the circumstances may be, God is still in control. And that you are able to believe, trust, and have faith enough in Him, depend on Him enough, have confidence in Him enough, to open your hands and mind to release the brakes that hinder. Yet to trust in Him enough, even when it may appear that He is leading you to where you would rather not go for now, but to know that eventually He will reveal the destiny He has planned just for you. And that you will trust in Him enough to respond as Habakkuk responded after he had seen the devastation, the violence, the disaster and ruin in Judah. And it appeared to him as if God had abandoned Judah. He cried out even when all seemed gloomy, "I will rejoice in the Lord." God is still God, whether He responds or answers, "Yes," "Delay," or "No" to our prayer now. To have this kind of faith that endures, and faith that releases our prayer brakes to transform our life, is reason enough to rejoice and be thankful to God.

Questions for Reflection

Instruction: React to the action strategies.

1. What are the action tips?

_____

_____

_____

_____

2. How do the action tips help you in your prayer life?

_____

_____

_____

_____

3. What did you learn about prayer?

_____

_____

_____

_____

4. Would you challenge a friend with the principles learned
   from this book? Why?

_____

_____

_____

_____

5. Would you take a leadership role to teach a class on
   prayer? Why?

_____

_____

_____

_____

References

Canfield, Jack; *How to Get from Where You Are to Where You Want to Be: The 25 Principles Of Success;* Harper Collins Publishers, London, 2007

Enyia, Samuel; *Creative Prayer Is Not For Showmanship;* Mass Communications Production and Graphic Design, South Holland, Illinois, 1994

Kriegel, J. Robert and Patler, Louis; *If it ain't Broke... BREAK IT! And Other Unconventional Wisdom for a Changing Business World;* Warner Books, A Time Warner Inc. Company, 1991.

Maxwell, John; *Running With The Giants: What Old Testament Heroes Want You To Know About Life And Leadership;* Warner Books, an AOL/Time Warner Company, 2007

Nouwen, Henri; ***With Open Hands;*** Ave Maria Press, Notre Dame, Indiana, 1997

Lightning Source UK Ltd.
Milton Keynes UK
UKHW011903240122
397637UK00002B/667